Library of
Davidson College

GLUCK AND HIS OPERAS.

GLUCK.

Gluck and his Operas, frontispiece.

GLUCK & HIS OPERAS

WITH AN ACCOUNT OF

THEIR RELATION TO MUSICAL ART

BY

HECTOR BERLIOZ

TRANSLATED FROM THE FRENCH BY

EDWIN EVANS, Senr.

Author of "Handbook to the Works of Brahms," "The Relation of Tchaikovsky to
Art Questions of the Day," "How to Compose," etc. Translator
of Wagner's "Oper und Drama" ("Opera and Drama").

GREENWOOD PRESS, PUBLISHERS
WESTPORT, CONNECTICUT

Library of Congress Cataloging in Publication Data

Berlioz, Hector, 1803-1869.
    Gluck & his operas.

    Reprint of the 1915 ed. published by W. Reeves,
London.
    1. Gluck, Christoph Willibald, Ritter von, 1714-
1787. I. Evans, Edwin, 1844-1923, tr. II. Title.
ML410.B5A543   1973   782.1'092'4   73-7695
ISBN 0-8371-6938-0

782.1
G567xb-T

Originally published in 1915 by Wm. Reeves, London

Reprinted by Greenwood Press, Inc.

First Greenwood reprinting 1973
Second Greenwood reprinting 1976

Library of Congress catalog card number 73-7695

ISBN 0-8371-6938-0

Printed in the United States of America

78-8953

PUBLISHER'S NOTE.

THESE essays and criticisms upon the operas of Gluck, together with the two companion volumes:

1. "A CRITICAL STUDY OF BEETHOVEN'S NINE SYMPHONIES"

    and

2. "MISCELLANEOUS ESSAYS UPON WAGNER, GOUNOD AND WEBER" (with addition of some fugitive sketches),

collectively comprise the great work by Hector Berlioz entitled

"A TRAVERS CHANTS"

ETUDES MUSICALES, ADORATIONS, BOUTADES ET CRITIQUES.

CONTENTS.

	PAGE
TRANSLATOR'S INTRODUCTION	ix

Gluck—His "Orphée."

ITS REPRESENTATION AT THE THÉÂTRE-LYRIQUE	1
OBSERVATIONS MADE AFTER THE FIRST PERFORMANCE	23

Gluck—His "Alceste."

THE "ALCESTE" OF EURIPIDES, AND THOSE OF QUINAULT AND CALSABIGI; THE SCORES OF LULLI, SCHWEIZER, GUGLIELMI AND HANDEL	37
INTRODUCTION	39
THE "ALCESTE" OF EURIPIDES	40
THE STORY OF "ALCESTE"	42
DIALOGUE BETWEEN PHÉRÈS AND ADMÈTE	43
REFLECTIONS ON THE DIALOGUE	46
THE "ALCESTE" OF QUINAULT	50
THE SCORE OF LULLI	56
GLUCK'S EARLY EXPERIENCES	58

CONTENTS.

	PAGE
GLUCK AND HIS ITALIAN SCORES	60
CALSABIGI'S LIBRETTO OF "ALCESTE"	63
GLUCK'S ACCOUNT OF HIS OWN SYSTEM	67
CRITICAL EXAMINATION OF GLUCK'S ACCOUNT	69
ANALYSIS OF GLUCK'S "ALCESTE"	75
THE SCORE OF GUGLIELMI	128
THE SCORE OF SCHWEIZER	134
THE SCORE OF HANDEL	137

The Revival of Gluck's "Alceste."

GENERAL DESCRIPTION	145
MADAME BRANCHU, ON THE CAREER OF THE FRENCH COMPOSER	153
THE REPRODUCTION	156
INDISPENSABLE CONDITIONS FOR THE PRODUCTION OF GREAT WORKS	163

PORTRAIT OF GLUCK . . . . . . *Frontispiece*

INTRODUCTION.

THE present portion of this work, though ostensibly an account of certain performances and revivals which took place in Paris round about the year 1860, is in reality an exhaustive study of Gluck; as interesting to the general reader as valuable to the student.

No one can be imagined so competent as Berlioz to handle this subject, and apart from intellectual qualifications few could approach it with such entire sympathy. This sympathy does not arise from any intensity of admiration on the part of Berlioz for Gluck's musicianship, the estimate of which contained in these pages certainly does not err upon the side of indulgence. Still less perhaps does it arise from any veneration for Gluck in having heroically carried out his schemes of opera-reform considering that herein the reader will find Gluck frequently reproached with failing to carry out his own principles. But it appertained to the warmth of Berlioz's nature to look over and beyond these weaknesses; and to regard only the general life-purpose by which Gluck was actuated, his immense intuition for dramatic effects and his extraordinary fertility of resource in giving effect to his intentions by a happy instrumentation.

The quality last alluded to is one which Berlioz himself possessed in an exceptional degree. Indeed, the view is at any rate partly justified that his reliance upon diversity of instrumentation occasionally exceeded what a correct balance between the various attributes of a composer would have necessitated. That being so, it becomes the more easy to understand why the novel orchestral effects of Gluck must have appealed to him with an irresistible force; and why the unity, consistency and life conferred upon the opera by that composer appeared to him as the very ideal of all that was true and noble in art.

It must not be supposed that, when Berlioz delivered the judgments upon "Orphée" and "Alceste" contained in these pages, the subject was new to him; and that the opinions expressed were merely the result of certain performances which he had recently attended. On the contrary, his treatise upon instrumentation, which had already been published for some years, abundantly testifies to the fact that many of the effects here so warmly described were already familiar to him; having been used for purposes of exemplification long before.*

The felicitous mode of expression which Berlioz naturally possessed, added to his copious knowledge and the extraordinary pains with which the present essays were evidently prepared, render the latter so well able to speak for themselves that "introduction," in the sense of any reference to their detail, is unnecessary. But it may be useful to refer to the general outline adopted which is one not only of very liberal dimensions, but which includes, in addition to the usual range of considerations forming part of a dissertation of this description, the treatment of a whole group of subjects bearing a subsidiary relation to the main objects of criticism.

First among these may be reckoned the account given of the divergence between the "Alceste" of Euripides and that of either Quinault, Calzabigi or Wieland. As a merely isolated circumstance the importance of this would, of course, be only measured by its influence upon the particular work in view. But it also relates to a question which is of far wider application; that, namely, of the treatment of classical subjects in any capricious manner which modern authors may

---

* The student-reader of these pages will derive much pleasure and instruction from a comparison of the examples from Gluck's "Orphée" and "Alceste" which are given in Berlioz's treatise on instrumentation with the descriptions herein contained of the dramatic situations to which they refer.

choose to adopt; and the boldness of Berlioz in extending his strictures so as even to include Racine's treatment of the Greek tragedies will afford the student much food for reflection.

A further extension of utility, due to this liberal outline, consists of the inclusion of a criticism of the scores of various other composers who, in one shape or other, have treated the subject of "Alceste." It will probably grate upon the feelings of some of Handel's admirers in this country to find him so lightly spoken of; but there would appear to be no escape from Berlioz's conclusions, the only attenuation of which lies in the fact that, with Handel, "Admetus" was a mere *pièce d'occasion;* whereas, with Gluck, it was an object of very special endeavour.

The extremely humorous castigation of Guglielmi may, at all events, be relied upon to atone for anything unwelcome in the foregoing. Here, again, Berlioz has so contrived his remarks as to invest them with a utility to the student extending far beyond the mere subject at issue. Whilst we laugh at the absurdities committed by Guglielmi, and which Berlioz so graphically describes, it is to the fate attending such attempts, and to the faithful way in which history repeats itself that our serious attention should be directed.

It will also be felt that the picture drawn by Berlioz of the Germanised Italian school of the period is eminently true to life; and that Schweizer, whether answering the description given of him in detail, or only to the extent of preparing discords, smoking tobacco, writing counterpoint and drinking beer, correctly represents the character *visé*. As for Lulli, although he is simply dismissed as a child, this does not happen without providing Berlioz with the occasion for valuable remarks upon the possibilities for effect afforded by simple means. Whether Berlioz himself was precisely the most appropriate person to read us a homily upon this subject may perhaps be questioned; but that reflection in no way affects the truth and value of his observations.

We see, therefore, that the ostensible object of these pages—that of giving an account of certain Paris performances—falls entirely into the background; and that they constitute, in reality, a most important essay upon the whole subject of Gluck's relation to musical art. Even the humorous anecdotes which are interspersed (by the fact that in spite of a superficial frivolity they have all a serious bearing upon the main subject) add to the musical value, as they do also to the literary excellence, of these pages. The same may be said of the various souvenirs by means of which Berlioz has succeeded in lightening the perusal while still pursuing the earnest course of his work.

Berlioz's mode of expression often causes the translator some hesitation between a literal rendering and the adoption of a slight freedom in order to ensure to the English reader the actual spirit of what was intended to be conveyed.

Such freedom has been however but sparingly exercised and limited to occasions where vagueness might otherwise have resulted. The reader may therefore regard the English dress in which these essays are now presented as one free of all adventitious feature.

EDWIN EVANS, Senior.

LONDON, *1914.*

GLUCK AND HIS OPERAS.

GLUCK'S "ORPHÉE" AND ITS REPRESENTATION AT THE THÉÂTRE-LYRIQUE.

IN the month of November, 1859, M. Carvalho, director of the Théâtre-Lyrique, ventured to undertake the reproduction of Gluck's "Orphée," and obtained by this audacity one of the greatest successes we have ever witnessed. It was, in fact, necessary not only to be bold; but also to be thoroughly convinced of the beauty of the work in question, to brave the prejudices of frivolous people, as well as the opposition of lovers of the commonplace, which soon rose up on all sides against his attempt. It was also requisite to turn a deaf ear to the recriminations of such people as were interested in showing themselves hostile to the revival of great works of art which they dread, as, immediately upon their production, the intelligent public begin to make crushing comparisons. Moreover, it was also necessary, with limited resources, to compass one of those faithful animated and living representations for want of which so many splendid works have been too often slandered, disfigured and destroyed.

At Paris, when one is in earnest and knows how to go about to make a good selection, there is no difficulty in forming an excellent orchestra, a satisfactory chorus, and in getting together a sufficiency of moderate singers to fulfil the subordinate parts in an opera; but, when it becomes a question of making sure of an artist of the first class for one of those great characters which will not tolerate anything imperfect or unworthy in their reproduction, the difficulty is nearly always insurmountable. It is to this class that "Orphée" belongs. Where shall we find a tenor uniting in himself all the special qualities demanded for the representation of this character? These include a profound acquaintance with the music; a skill in the broader style of singing; complete command of the simple and severe style; a powerful and noble voice; profound sensibility; facial expression; beauty and ease of gesture; and, finally, a perfect comprehension and intelligent appreciation of the work of Gluck.

Fortunately, the director of the Théâtre-Lyrique was aware that the part of Orphée had been originally written for a contralto; and he therefore felt that, in securing its acceptance by Madame Viardot, he was assuring the success of his enterprise. In this he succeeded; and, when once sure of the co-operation of this great artist, he submitted the score to the special operations which we are now about to describe. Now

"ORFEO ED EURIDICE"
AZIONE THEATRALE PER LA MUSICA DEL SIGNOR CRISTOFANO GLUCK

was originally an opera in three very short acts, the Italian text of which had been written by Calzabigi. It was given for the first time at Vienna in 1764; soon afterwards at Parma, and, subsequently, at numerous other theatres in Italy.

At Vienna, the cast was as follows:

Orfeo, Signor Gaetano Guadagni (contralto-castrato).
Eurydice, Signora Marianna Bianchi.
Amore, Signora Lucia Clavarau.

The name has even been preserved of the ballet-master, Gasparo Angiolini; as well as that of the stage-manager, Maria Quaglio.

Later on, Gluck, having come to France for the purpose of producing "Orphée" at the Royal Academy, had Calzabigi's libretto translated by M. Molines; he transposed the leading part for the high tenor voice of Legros; added several numbers to the score; and applied a series of important modifications to the remainder.

Among the new numbers thus introduced we need only mention;

(1) The first air of Cupid:

> Si les doux accords de ta lyre;[1]

(2) That of Eurydice with chorus:

> Cette asile aimable et tranquille;[2]

(3) The bravura song which the composer introduced at the end of the first act:

> L'Espoir renaît dans mon âme;[3]

(4) The pantomime flute solo, in the first scene of the Elysian fields;

(5) And several highly-developed "airs de ballet."

Besides that, he added six bars to the first song of Orphée in the infernal scene; three in the second; three to the peroration of the air:

> Che faro senza Euridice;[4]

and one only to the chorus of happy shades:

> Torna o bella al tuo consorte.[5]

(He was rather late in perceiving that the absence of this bar destroyed the regularity of the final phrase.)

He almost completely re-instrumented the delightful descriptive symphony which serves as an accompaniment to the song of Orphée at his entrance into the Elysian fields:

> Che puro ciel! che chiaro sol![6]

---

[1] If the sweet accents of thy lyre.
[2] This pleasant and tranquil shelter.
[3] Hope dawns again in my soul.
[4] What shall I do without Eurydice!
[5] Turn, O fair one, to thy consort.
[6] How pure the sky, how bright the sun.

he suppressed more than forty bars in the recitative which begins the third act; and he entirely remodelled another one.

These improvements, as well as some others which I omit here to mention, were all to the advantage of the score. Unfortunately, other corrections were also made, probably by a strange hand; by which certain passages were mutilated in the most barbarous fashion. These mutilations have been preserved in the published French score and were always observed at the performances of "Orphée" which I heard so often at the opera, from 1825 to 1830.

At the time when Gluck wrote "Orfeo" at Vienna, an instrument was in use, which is still employed to accompany the chorals at some churches in Germany, and which he calls "cornetto." It is made of wood, is pierced with holes, and is played with an embouchure either of copper or horn; similar to the embouchure of the trumpet.

In the religious funeral ceremony which takes place round the tomb of Eurydice, in the first act of "Orfeo," Gluck adds the "cornetto" to the three trombones, in order to accompany the four chorus parts. The "cornetto" not being known at the Opera of Paris, was later on suppressed without being replaced by any other instrument; and the sopranos of the chorus, whose part it followed in unison in the Italian score, were thus deprived of instrumental support. In the third verse of the romance of the first act:

> Piango il mio ben cosi

the composer introduced two cors anglais; but, as the orchestra at the Opera did not possess these instruments, they were replaced by two clarinets.

For the contralto voices, which are of such happy effect in the choruses, and which Gluck employed in "Orfeo" after the manner of all Italian and German masters, the Paris management substituted noisy high tenor voices. Moreover, in the chorus of the Elysian fields:

> Viens dans ce séjour paisible,[7]

at the passage where the coryphées sing:

> Eurydice va paraître [8]

and which is so well written in the Italian score, this high tenor part was modified without anyone being able to understand why; and in such an unfortunate manner as, four times, to commit a fault of harmony of the worst possible description.

As to the faults of engraving existing in both the French and Italian scores; the essential indications they omit; and the marks of expression ill-placed in them; I should never finish their description.

Gluck seems to have been extremely idle; and re-

---

[7] Come into this peaceful sojourn.
[8] Eurydice will now appear.

markably careless in revising his most beautiful compositions, not merely with the harmonic correctness worthy of a master, but even with the ordinary care to be expected from a good copyist. Often, in order not to give himself the trouble of writing the orchestral viola part, he indicates it by the words:

Col basso,

without noticing that, as the result of this direction, the viola part, naturally two octaves higher than that of the double-bass, would rise above the first violins. In some places (in the last chorus of the happy shades, for instance) he has written the viola part out fully in this way; in such a manner as to produce "octaves" between the extreme parts of the harmony; a mere school-boy fault, which it is as surprising as it is distressing to find in such a place.

Finally, trombone parts were added, by one of the old leaders of the Opera orchestra, for certain parts of the infernal scene, where the composer had not supplied them; and this of course weakened the effect of their intervention at the famous answer of the demons:

"Non!"

in which the composer had desired to make them heard.

It may be conceived from the above how extensive was the labour to be incurred in order to restore this work to a proper condition; to render the recitatives and new airs, added by Gluck to the principal part on the occasion of its transformation into a tenor "Orphée," suitable for a contralto voice; to remove the trombone parts, which had been added by a stranger, as well as to replace, by a modern cornet of brass, the "cornetto" of wood which no one plays in Paris, and which doubles the sopranos of the chorus, going with the trombone group in the first and second acts.

Besides all this, some lines had to be corrected in the libretto of M. Molines; as their stupidity seemed dangerous and unacceptable, even to a public so accustomed to the "Molines" class of poet.

Was it possible, for instance, to allow Eurydice to say, when she wishes to attract the attention of her spouse:

"Contente mon envie!"[9]

and a few more beauties of the same sort?

* * *

After this long preamble, which was necessary however, we shall be more at ease in speaking of Gluck's "Orphée"; and of the way in which it has been reproduced at the Théâtre-Lyrique.

M. Janin recently observed that "it is not we who are again taking up the masterpieces; it is rather they which are taking us up."

---

[9] "Satisfy my wish,"

It may truly be said that "Orphée" has taken us up—all of us, that is, who are well disposed. As to the others—as to those of the "Polonius" class, who of course find everything too long, and who can only be kept awake by a risky story, or a dirty parody, no masterpiece wants anything to do with them; and "Orphée" would certainly have no inclination to take *them* up.

We know that; and yet we feel distressed in listening to the various opinions of the vulgar crowd, every time an important artistic production is submitted to its judgment. We are liable to feel all the more distressed, if, after experiencing noble emotions, we happen to hear the probable *cash result* discussed of the work by which our feelings have been moved; or, if the infamous phrase: "Will that make money?" should chance to be repeated in our presence.

But, rather than embark upon these questions of lucre and traffic to which everything nowadays is unfortunately submitted, let us proceed to treat frankly of those things which appeal to us inwardly; and thus avoid giving ourselves pain in order that we may have pleasure. What is genius? What is glory? What is the beautiful? I do not know; and neither you, monsieur, nor you, madame, know it any better than I. But what seems certain to me is that, if an artist has been able to produce a work capable of rousing at all times elevated sentiments and refined passion; and if his work effects this in the hearts of that class of men whom we believe, by the delicacy of their organism and the culture of their minds, to be superior to others; then undoubtedly it follows that that artist has genius; that he merits glory; and that what he has produced deserves to be called beautiful.

Such an artist was Gluck. His "Orphée" is now nearly a century old; and, after an age of evolutions, revolutions and diverse agitations, both in art and the world at large, this work has recently profoundly "touched and charmed the public of the Théâtre-Lyrique. It cannot matter after that what may be the views of people of the class of Shakespeare's Polonius; whose mental condition necessitates a racy story to keep them awake. The affection and passion for art resemble love; for we love simply because we love, and without taking the least account of the more or less disastrous consequences attached to it.

Yes, the immense majority of the audience at the first representation of "Orphée" experienced sincere admiration for the traits of genius so frequently met with in this old score. They found the choruses of the introduction to be of a sombre character perfectly consistent with the drama, and distinctly emotional by the very slowness of their rhythm and the sad solemnity of their melody; and that the sorrowful cry of Orphée:

"Eurydice!"

raised at intervals in the middle of lamentations by

the chorus, was a distinctly admirable trait. The music of the romance:

> Objet de mon amour,
> Je te demande un jour
> Avant l'aurore.

is a worthy translation of the lines of Virgil:

> Te dulcis conjux, te solo in littore secum,
> Te veniente die, te decedente canebat.

The recitatives, by which the two verses of this number are preceded and followed, have a truth of accent and an elegance of form which are extremely rare. The distant orchestra, placed in the coulisse, and repeating, as an echo, the conclusion of each phrase of the forlorn poet, renders the sorrowful charm greater still. The first air of Cupid has a certain malicious grace, such as is commonly attributed to the god of Paphos; but the second contains several set forms of rather questionable taste—forms which, on that account, have become antiquated. The "bravura-song" has become even more so; but let us hasten to say that the specimen of the latter which occurs in "Orphée" is not by Gluck. This number, the presence of which in the score of such a work seems inexplicable, is taken from an opera, called "Tancrède," composed by an obscure Italian master, named Bertoni; to whom we shall shortly allude. In the "acte des Enfers" the instrumental introduction; the air of the Furies; the chorus of demons, threatening at first, but gradually soothed until finally subdued by the voice of Orphée; as well as the heartrending and withal melodious supplications of the latter—everything is sublime.

What marvellous music, too, is that of the Elysian fields; with its vaporous harmonies, expressive of a placid happiness; and with its sweet and feeble instrumentation, so well rendering the idea of an infinite peace! All this seems to caress and fascinate the listener; causing in him a distaste for the coarser sensations of life, and the yearning for an existence in which he could eternally enjoy the divine murmur.

How many people there are who blush to allow their emotion to be seen; and yet have had to shed tears, in spite of all effort to restrain them, at the last chorus of this act:

Près du tendre objet qu'on aime;[10]

as well as at the sweet monologue of Orphée, describing the scene of his happy sojourn:

Quel nouveau ciel pare ces lieux![1]

Further beauties are encountered in the duet, full of desperate agitation; the tragic accents of the great air of Eurydice; the melodious theme of that of Orphée:

J'ai perdu mon Eurydice,[2]

interspersed with episodial slow movements of the

---

[10] Near the tender object of our love.
[1] How changed is the sky which decks this place!
[2] I have lost my Eurydice.

most poignant expression; and the short but admirable largo:

Oui, je te suis, cher objet de ma foi,[3]

in which the sentiment of ecstatic joy of the lover who is about to die in order to rejoin his beloved is so well recognised; all these things contribute worthily to crown this beautiful antique poem which Gluck has bequeathed to us, and upon the grace and expressive force of which ninety-five years have had no effect.

I believe I said just now that the instrumentation had only been retouched for the present revival so far as was necessary in order to restore it to its original condition.

Mlle. Marimon is graceful in the part of Cupid; but she exhibits an occasional desire to drag the time, which we advise her in future to endeavour to avoid. She should remember that the character she represents is that of the winged god of Paphos and of Gnide; and not that of the goddess of wisdom.

Mlle. Moreau (the happy Shade) had to repeat the air with chorus:[4]

Cet asile aimable et tranquille,[5]

which requires a high soprano, and which she sang with

---

[3] Yes, I follow thee, dear object of my faith.

[4] This air belongs to the part of Eurydice in the score (author's note).

[5] Already referred to, page 4.

purity. Of Mlle. Sax it may be said that she puts much energy—possibly even a little too much—into the part of the beloved of "Orphée." Eurydice, it must be remembered, is a timid and gentle young woman; whose manner of singing is quite inconsistent with great vocal outbursts. Nevertheless, the performance by Mlle. Sax was extremely good in the case of the air:

Fortune ennemie.

To speak, now, of Madame Viardot is to approach what forms a study in itself. Her talent is so complete and varied; it touches so many points of art; and is united to so much science, and to such an entrancing spontaneity, that it produces, at one and the same time, both astonishment and emotion; the result being that it strikes, and yet appeals to the heart; it overawes, and yet persuades. Her voice, which is of exceptional compass, is at the service of a consummate skill in vocalisation and of an equal art in phrasing the broader kind of song, both of which are extremely rare at the present time. She unites an irrepressibly impetuous and imperious verve with a profound sensibility and an almost painfully truthful faculty for the expression of immense grief. Her gesture is well moderated, being both noble and true to nature; and the expression of her face, always powerful, is even more so in the dumb scenes than in those in which it merely aids the accentuation of song.

At the opening of the first act of "Orphée" her

graceful attitudes at the tomb of Eurydice recall those of certain characters in the landscapes of Poussin; or, rather, certain bas-reliefs that Poussin took for his models. The virile antique costume, moreover, suits her uncommonly well.

Madame Viardot had no sooner arrived at her first recitative:

> Aux mânes sacrés d'Eurydice
> Rendez les suprêmes honneurs,
> Et couvrez son tombeau de fleurs [6]

than she took complete possession of her audience. Each word—each note had its effect. The great and beautiful melody:

> Objet de mon amour [7]

delivered with an incomparable breadth of style, and a grief profoundly calm, was several times interrupted by exclamations of pleasure, which escaped the most impressionable among the audience. Nothing could be more graceful than her gesture, or more touching than her voice, when she turns to the scene, saying, as she contemplates the trees of the sacred wood:

> Sur ces troncs dépouillés de l'écorce naissante,
> On lit ce mot, gravé par une main tremblante: [8]

To the sacred shade of Eurydice render supreme honour and cover her tomb with flowers.
[7] Already referred to, page 11.
[8] Upon these trunks, despoiled of the growing bark
We read the word, engraved by a trembling hand.

There is elegy; there is antique idyll: it is Theocritus—it is Virgil.

But, at the cry:

> Implacables tyrans, j'irai vous la ravir.[9]

all changes; reverie and grief giving way to enthusiasm and passion. Orpheus, seizing his lyre, is about to descend into hell:

> Les monstres du Ténare ne l'épouvantent pas;[10]

and, in realisation of his resolve to bring back Eurydice, to describe what Mme. Viardot made of this bravura piece is well nigh impossible. In listening to it one does not think of style; for the reason that the listener is, as it were, seized and carried along by a torrent of impetuous vocalisation; precisely what is required by the situation.

It is well known in what manner Mme. Viardot sings the "infernal scene"; which she has so often performed, both in London and Paris. But never, as may be supposed, has she united the full ardour of supplication with emotional quivering of the voice and expiring tones so as to give such reality to the soothing of the ghosts and spectres and infernal monsters.

But here it is that the talent of the actress is proved with the greatest force of evidence. We are now in the sojourn of eternal peace. Moved by the song of

---

[9] Implacable tyrants, I shall go to wrest her from you.
[10] The monsters of Tænarus do not daunt him.

Orphée, the shades, mere phantoms deprived of life, come from the depths of Erebus in crowds as numerous as the thousands of birds who hide themselves in the surrounding foliage:

> Matres, atque viri, defuncta que corpora vita
> Magnanimum heroum, pueri innuptæque puellæ.

The question for the great artist was to rise to the height of Virgil's poetical expression; and right well she succeeded.

Nothing could be more solemn than her entrance into that part of Elysium which the shades have just abandoned; nothing more sweetly grave than those beautiful contralto tones which one hears, audibly exhaled from the depth of the scene, in the midst of the solitude, and during the harmonious murmur of waters and foliage; at the words:

> Quel nouveau ciel parc ces lieux.[11]

But the beloved one does not appear; where shall she be found? Orphée becomes uneasy; the smile which played upon his lips now disappears. He calls: "Eurydice! Eurydice!" whereupon the younger shades appear. There they come: the young belles; sweethearts and virgins:

> innuptæ puellæ

in groups of twos and threes, arm in arm, with head

---

[11] See also page 12

slightly inclined upon the shoulder; and with inquisitive eyes turned in silence towards the living. Orphée, becoming more and more anxious, goes from group to group, examining those beautiful young pale faces; and hoping to recognise that of Eurydice but always deceived in the expectation. Discouragement and fear get the better of him at last; and he is about to give way to despair when voices are heard, issuing from a grove not far away, singing that ineffable melody:

> Eurydice va paraître
> Avec de nouveaux attraits.[1]

His joy then reappears; his smiles being mingled with tears, as is usual in moments of such supreme delight; and the shades are perceived at last, leading the sweetly beloved one:

> dulcis conjux.

Orphée, without turning round, and without seeing her, but warned of her approach by a mysterious sense of ecstasy and great love, commences to tremble; when, the hand of Eurydice being placed in his, he staggers at the adored contact, is breathing heavily and is upon the point of fainting. He moves away, however, with an uncertain step; taking Eurydice, still cold and astonished, with him; and thus he mounts the hill which leads to the heaven of the living, whilst the shades, motionless and silent, hold out their arms from

---

[1] See also page 6.

below, as a sign of last adieu to the two lovers. What a picture! What music! and what acting of Mme. Viardot! It is sublime in its grace, the ideal of love and divinely beautiful.

Oh, to belong to the Polonius class of mortals and have no heart to appreciate such beauty. What a pitiable fate.

We have still much to admire; even without speaking of the sorrowful agitation with which Mme. Viardot delivers the entire part of Orphée in the grand duet:

> Viens, suis un époux qui t'adore ;[2]

or, of her attitude and accent at her "aside" in the other duet; where, upon a heartrending chromatic progression, the words occur:

> Que mon sort est à plaindre ![3]

It remains to mention the culminating triumph of the great artist in this *creation* of the part of Orphée; I mean, her execution of the celebrated air:

> J'ai perdu mon Eurydice.[4]

Gluck has somewhere said, "change the slightest shade of movement or of accent in that air, and you make a dance of it."

Mme. Viardot makes of it precisely what it is wanted to be; one of those prodigies of expression, wellnigh

---

[2] Come, follow a spouse who adores thee.
[3] How pitiable is my lot.
[4] See also page 2.

incomprehensible for vulgar singers, and which are, alas! so often profaned. She delivered the theme in three different ways: firstly, with a contained grief, and in slow movement; then, after the episodial adagio:

> Mortel silence!
> Vaine espérance![5]

in *sotto voce, pianissimo*, and with a trembling voice choked by a flood of tears; and, finally, after the second adagio, she took the theme with a more animated movement, in quitting the body of Eurydice by the side of which she had been kneeling, and in throwing herself, mad with despair, towards the opposite side of the scene, with the bitter cries and sobs of a distracted grief.

I shall not try to describe the transports of the audience at this overpowering scene; though I may mention that some ignorant admirers forgot themselves so far as to call "encore!" before the sublime passage:

> Entends ma voix qui t'appelle;[6]

and there was even some trouble in inducing them to be quiet. There are some people who would equally call "encore!" for the scene of Priam in the tent of Achilles; or, for the soliloquy, "to be or not to be" in "Hamlet." But why, after so much praise, should it now be necessary to reproach Mme. Viardot with a

---

[5] Deathly silence! vain hope!
[6] Dost hear my voice, which calleth thee?

deplorable feature of her performance, occurring at the end of this air? It consists of a change, produced by a holding note which she makes upon the high G, and which obliges the orchestra to stop, instead of proceeding precipitously towards the conclusion, as Gluck had written; and which also leads to a modification of the harmony, as well as to the substitution of the chord of the dominant for that of the sixth upon the subdominant: in short, it is the contrary of what Gluck intended. Why should there also be some textual alterations; and a few misplaced roulades in a recitative to reproach her with? Alas, why!

The style of production, as already observed, is worthy of the work. Nothing more ingenious or more consistent with the subject (especially for the Elysian fields and for the infernal scene) could be imagined. The costumes, moreover, are charming, and the dances sufficient; so that, upon the whole, this revival of Gluck's poetic score reflects the greatest honour upon Monsieur Carvalho, and entitles him to the gratitude of every friend of art.

GLUCK.

HIS "ORPHÉE" AT THE THÉÂTRE-LYRIQUE.

Observations made after the first performance.

GLUCK.

HIS "ORPHÉE" AT THE THÉÂTRE-LYRIQUE.

Observations made after the first performance.

"ORPHÉE" begins to have a vogue which is rather disquieting; and we hope, at all events, that Gluck is not going to be in fashion. Let the theatre be full at every performance of the masterpiece; by all means. Let Monsieur Carvalho make plenty of money, by all means. Let the musical manners of the Parisians purify themselves, and let their microscopic ideas get a little bigger and rise a little higher; by all possible means. And let the artistic public settle down to an exceptional delight; by all means; emphatically, by all means. But, should the entire "Polonius" class (that being the new name of Monsieur Prud'homme) now feel obliged to remain awake at the representations of "Orphée"? Ought they to be constrained to hide themselves when they want to go to their favourite parodies in a theatre which it is forbidden to name? And, is it right that they should have to pretend to find Gluck's music charming? By *no* means! By *no* means! Why should they seek to drive away what is natural to them? especially considering that it is quite sure to come back with a gallop. Why should anyone who is a respectable Monsieur Prud'homme, or a Polonius (with or without a beard) not speak his usual language instead of pretending to understand and feel? Why should he not say frankly, like ordinary people: "What a bore!" "Oh! what a bore!"? (I do not quote the exact expression in use by Messrs. "Polonius" as it is not quite recognised in literature). Why should they lower their voices at all to express what we have so often heard declared outright: "Excuse me, madam, to have inflicted this rhapsody upon you; or, made you come to this funereal business; we are going to see Punch and Judy in the Champs-Elysées for consolation. We consider that we have been robbed; yes, robbed, in the full strength of the term and just as we might have been in the middle of the forest of Bondy. It is those stupid critics who have lured us into this trap."

Or, on the other hand: "This is very learned music, very learned; but, if it is necessary to study counterpoint in order to enjoy it, you will admit, my dear Mme. Prud'homme, that it is beyond our means."

Or, again: "There are not two bars of melody in the whole of it; and, if we young composers were to write such music, we should have potatoes thrown at us."

Or, again: "That is music made by calculation; and it is only good for mathematicians."

Or, again: "That is fine; but very long."

Or, again: "It is both long and good for nothing"; besides a good many more aphorisms equally worthy of admiration.

Yes, it would be a pity if this new kind of hypocrisy were to spread; for nothing is more pleasing or flattering for people organised in a proper way than to see the things they love and admire insulted by those who are organised otherwise. It is the complement of their happiness; and, in the opposite case, they might be tempted to paraphrase the aside of an ancient orator and say: Since the "Polonius" class appear to be so pleased, we shall have to feign an admiration for rubbish.

But we need not disturb ourselves; for this is not going to happen. Gluck will not be in fashion; and, for the last few days, the Punch and Judy receipts have steadily gone up; on account of the increase in the number of people who have gone to see the show for consolation.

* * * * * *

One important feature of the excellent effect produced at the Théâtre-Lyrique by the work of Gluck must be attributed to the modest dimensions of the building; which allow both the words, which are so intimately united to the music generally and to the delicacy of the instrumentation in particular to be heard. I consider that I have elsewhere proved that rooms which are too vast are fatal to the refinements, and to the most intimate charms, of art. It is these vast spaces which have caused the introduction into opera libretti of so much in the way of nonsense and audacious stupidity; which the perpetrators of these things seek to justify by saying that they are *not heard*. It is these vast spaces (I shall never tire of repeating it) which seem to excuse certain composers for the insensate brutalities of their orchestra. These same vast spaces have also contributed to produce the school of singing which we now enjoy, and in which, instead of singing, it is considered right to vociferate; in which, in order to give more force to the emission of the sound, the singer takes breath for every four, and often for every three notes; thus breaking up and destroying every well-built phrase and every noble melody; suppressing the elisions; making frequent lines of thirteen or fourteen feet, without counting either the splitting up of the musical rhythm, or the hiatus or the hundred other villainies, which transform melody into recitative, verse into prose and French into the patois of Auvergne. It is these "money-gulfs" which have always brought about the howlings of tenors, basses and sopranos at the Opera; and have caused the most famous singers of that theatre to merit the titles of bulls, peacocks and guinea fowls, which coarse people are accustomed to give them, as such folk do not trouble to call things otherwise than by their correct names.

On this very subject one of Gluck's sayings is quoted, as having taken place at the Royal Academy of Music during a rehearsal of "Orphée"; when Legros was persisting in shouting, according to his method, the phrase relating to the entry into Tartarus:

> Laissez-vous toucher par mes pleurs![1]

At last the composer became exasperated; and, interrupting him in the middle of the period, treated him to the following blunt attack:

"Monsieur! Monsieur! Be good enough to moderate your clamour. By the very devil they don't cry out like that, even in hell."

> Comme avec irréverénce
> Parlait aux dieux ce maraud![2]

And yet they were already far removed from the good old time when Lulli broke his violin on the head of a bad player, and when Handel threw a recalcitrant lady singer out of the window. But Gluck was protected by his gracious pupil, the Queen of France, and Vestris, the "god" of the dance, having dared to say that one could not dance to Gluck's "airs de ballet," found himself obliged to go and apologise to Chevalier Gluck, by order of Marie Antoinette. It is even related that

---

[1] Let your hearts be softened at my tears.
[2] See with what irreverence that rascal spoke to the gods

this interview was of a most agitated description. Gluck was tall and strong; and, seeing the light little "god" come into the room, he ran towards him, took him under the arms, and, singing a dance tune from "Iphigenia in Aulide," danced him willy-nilly right round the apartment. Afterwards, deposing him breathless upon a seat, he said to him with a sneer:

"Ah! Ah! You see that my 'airs de ballet' are uncommonly good to dance to; since, only to hear me hum one of them, makes you jump about like a kid."

The Théâtre-Lyrique has the dimensions which are most suitable for the complete effect of such a work as "Orphée." Nothing is lost in it; neither the sounds of the orchestra, nor those of the voices, nor the facial expression of the actors.

* * * * * *

In regard to "Orphée" I shall here mention one of the most audacious plagiarisms of which there is any example in the history of music, and which I discovered a few years ago in going through a score by Philidor. This learned musician had had the proofs of the Italian score of "Orfeo" through his hands, as we know. It was published in Paris, during the absence of the composer; and Philidor seems to have thought the occasion appropriate for purloining the melody of

Objet de mon amour [3]

---

[3] See also pages 11 and 15.

and for adopting it in some indifferent way to the words of a number of his own opera, "Le Sorcier," which he was then writing. All he did was to change bars one, five, six, seven and eight; and transform the first period, which Gluck had composed as three times three bars, into another formed of twice four bars; because the metre of his own text compelled him to do so. But, from the point where the words occur:

> Dans son cœur on ne sent éclore
> Que le seul désir de se voir,[4]

Philidor simply copied Gluck's melody; bass, harmony and even the echoes of the oboe in his little orchestra placed at the wings; transposing the whole into the key of A. I have never heard this impudent theft spoken of; but it is one which will appear manifest to anyone who will cast his eyes upon the romance of Bastien:

> Nous étions dans cet âge,

on page 33 of the score of "Le Sorcier."

I now learn that, M. de Sévelinges having already mentioned it in an account of Philidor published by him in Michaud's "Universal Biography," M. Fétis evinced some desire to defend the French musician. Now, the first representation of "Orfeo" is supposed to have taken place at Vienna in the course of 1764; and, that of "Le Sorcier" having occurred at Paris on

---

[4] In his heart the only feeling is the increasing desire to meet.

January the second of the same year, it seemed impossible to Fétis that Philidor could have known anything about Gluck's work. But M. Farrenc has recently proved by authentic documents that "Orfeo" was first played at Vienna in 1762; that Favart was entrusted with the publication of the score in Paris in 1763; and that, at this very time, Philidor *offered* himself to correct the proofs and *inspect the engraving* of the work.

It seems to me, therefore, most likely that this officious proof-corrector, after having stolen Gluck's romance, himself changed the date from 1762 to that of 1764, on the title page of the score of "Orfeo"; in order to render plausible the following argument; the very one which this false date naturally suggested to M. Fétis:

"Philidor cannot have stolen from Gluck, because 'Le Sorcier' was played before 'Orfeo.'"

But the fact of the theft is supported by such positive evidence as to make it clear that, with only a little more audacity, Philidor would have caused Gluck himself to pass for being the thief.

I now return to the bravura song which closes the first act of "Orphée" in the French score. I had heard that it was not by Gluck, who, however, has written airs of this kind in several of his Italian scores; and I wanted to assure myself about this. After having searched in vain at the library of the conservatoire for the score of "Tancrède," by Bertoni, from which they said it had been taken, I finished by finding it at the Imperial Library; and, in turning over the pages of the first act of this work, I recognised the piece in question at a first glance. It is impossible, in fact, to mistake it; merely a few notes having been added, in the "Orphée" version, to its ritornello.

Now, how did this air become introduced into Gluck's opera? And who did it? That is precisely what I do not know. But, in a French pamphlet written by a man called Coquian, who was an antagonist of Gluck, and which, under the title:

Entretiens sur l'état actuel de l'opéra de Paris,

was published in Paris in 1779, the great composer is violently attacked and accused of several plagiarisms; particularly of having stolen one entire air from a score by Bertoni. The partisans of Gluck having denied the fact, Coquian wrote to Bertoni; from whom he received the following answer, which he published in a supplement to his pamphlet, calling it:

Suite des entretiens sur l'état actuel de l'opéra de Paris;

or "Letters to M. S." (Suard).

Notwithstanding the circumspection and embarrassment of the Italian musician, as well as his comical fear about compromising himself, the truth appears none the less, and, in fact, superabundantly in this letter; the communication of which we owe to the kindness of M. Anders, of the Imperial Library. It is as follows:

> LONDON,
> *September 9, 1779.*
>
> SIR,
>
> I am very surprised to find myself challenged in the letter with which you honour me, and I should strongly desire not to be compromised in a musical quarrel; which, by the warmth of feeling you put into it, is capable of becoming of very great consequence, since you assure me that fanaticism is mixed up in it, which is another reason for me to withdraw from its effects. I shall beg you therefore to permit me to answer you simply that the air
>
> "S'oche dal ciel discende"
>
> was composed by me at Turin, for Signora Girelli; I do not recollect in what year, and I could not tell you whether I did it really for "Iphiginia in Tauride" as you assure me. I should rather think that it belongs to my opera of "Tancrède," but that does not prevent the air being mine. The above is what I can certify as a man of honour, full of respect for the works of the great masters; but full of tenderness for his own. It is with these sentiments that I remain,
>
> Sir, your obedient servant,
> FERDINAND BERTONI.[5]

"Tancrède" was played at Venice during the carnival of 1767; and the French "Orphée" was not represented in Paris until 1774. Probably the singer Legros, who created the part of Orphée at Paris, not being satisfied with the simple recitative with which Calsabigi and Gluck had finished their first act, wanted

---

[5] On account of Bertoni's imperfect acquaintance with the French language some mistakes occur in the above letter; which, though faithfully given in Berlioz's version, would have no interest for the English reader (translator's note).

Gluck to provide a bravura piece. Gluck, being disinclined to write one, but yielding to Legros's request, very likely said to him, in giving him this air by Bertoni:

"Here you are! Take that and sing it; and let me alone!"

But this does not justify Gluck in having allowed Bertoni's air to be printed in his score, without indicating the source from which he had taken it. Neither does it explain his keeping silence during the time that the author of the pamphlet of which I have just spoken was denouncing the plagiarism.

It is as well to mention that this Bertoni, now so unknown, had, in 1766, brought out the "Orfeo" of Calsabigi at the theatre of San Benedetto at Venice; on which occasion he appears to have rewritten the music.

In publishing his score (which I have read) he finds it necessary to excuse himself for such boldness. He says:

"I neither pretend nor hope to obtain for my 'Orfeo' a success to be compared with that which has just welcomed the masterpiece of M. Gluck all over Europe; and, if I can only merit the encouragement of my fellow-countrymen, I shall esteem myself happy."

He had good reason to be modest; for his music is, as it were, "traced over" that of Gluck. In several places (and especially in the Infernal Scene) the rhythmical forms of the German master are so faithfully imitated that, if one looks at the score from a certain distance, the aspect of the groups of notes becomes deceptive, and it is easy to imagine one's self looking at the "Orphée" of Gluck.

May it not be that Gluck said to himself, when the question of the air from "Tancrède" was mentioned:

"This Italian has robbed me enough for his 'Orfeo'; surely, I can have an air from him in my turn."

This is possible; but it is too unworthy of such a man to make us very ready to believe it. Anyhow, the above is all I know about the whole circumstance.

* * * * * *

When Adolphe Nourrit took the part of Orphée at the Opera he suppressed the bravura song; either on account of the piece not pleasing him, or because he knew of the fraud; and replaced it by a very beautiful agitated air, taken from "L'Écho et Narcisse," by Gluck:

O transport, ô désordre extrême!

the words and music of which, happily, chance to fit the situation. This, I think, is what should be always done.

GLUCK.

HIS "ALCESTE."

The "Alceste" of Euripides; that of Quinault and Calsabigi; also the scores of Lulli, Schweizer, Guglielmi and Handel.

GLUCK.

HIS "ALCESTE."

The "Alceste" of Euripides; that of Quinault and Calsabigi; also the Scores of Lulli, Schweizer, Guglielmi and Handel.

INTRODUCTION.

THE tragedy of "Alceste," by Euripides, has formed the subject of several operas; one by Quinault, set to music by Lulli; another by Calsabigi, set to music by Gluck; another by Wieland, set to music by Schweizer; and a few others. That of Gluck, first written to an Italian text for the Opera at Vienna, was afterwards translated into French, with some modifications, for the Royal Academy of Music of Paris; and enriched by Gluck with several important numbers. As none of these lyrical works completely resembles the Greek tragedy, it will probably be useful, on the present occasion of the reproduction of Gluck's monumental work, to examine the original ancient piece, upon which all these modern productions are based.

THE "ALCESTE" OF EURIPIDES.

The tragedy of Euripides would, nowadays, shock the manners, ideas and sentiments of any civilised nation. In reading it, with merely slight attention, we might imagine a professor of rhetoric saying to his pupils: "This is a farce"; so much have manners changed, on the one hand; and so much has literary education, and that of France especially, taken the direction, on the other, of causing whatever is natural and true to be disliked. We ought, however, to reflect that the Athenians were neither barbarians nor fools; and not be too ready to think it probable that they could, in literature, have admired and applauded monstrosities and impertinences.

In the case of Euripides, as in that of Shakespeare, we are evidently inclined to stipulate that the poet should take our present habits into account. Not only our habits; but even our religious beliefs and prejudices, as well as our new vices, are expected to be reckoned with; and we even absurdly require to make a great effort of literary probity and good sense, before we can recognise the simple fact that a great poet, living at Athens two thousand years ago, and writing for a people whose language and whose religion is imperfectly known to us, could scarcely propose to himself to obtain the suffrages of Parisians in the year 1861.

This, however, merely relates to the groundwork of

the question; and our reflections should further embrace the fact that the great Greek poets, who wrote in perhaps the most harmonious language which men have ever spoken, are fatally and inevitably disfigured by unfaithful translators. These men are very often incapable even of understanding the original Greek; and at all times they find themselves in the impossibility of transferring the harmony of style, or even so much as the images and thoughts, of the original into our modern languages; which not only lack colour, but are beset by a prudery difficult to reconcile with the true expression of certain sentiments.

The Latin poets are very much in the same position. Who would dare nowadays, even if he could, to translate faithfully into French those touching and simple words of the Didon[1] of Virgil:

> Si quis mihi parvulus aula
> Luderet Æneas, qui te tamen ore referret;

a translation of which would now only provoke laughter. "A little Énée," they would say, "a little Énée, playing in my yard!" What is he playing with? with a hoop, or a top? The humorous feature in such questions is that in a certain literary world they sincerely believe that they have made the acquaintance of ancient poems through modern translations and imitations; so that many people would be quite astonished

---

[1] Classical proper names as in the original French.

to have it proved to them that Bitaubé no more gives an idea of Homer, than the Abbé Delille gives of Virgil; or than Racine does of the Greek tragedies.

This reserve being made with regard to translators (who are necessarily the most perfidious people in the world) let us see what Père Brumoy condescends to show us of the "Alceste" of Euripides; or, at least, of the succession of scenes which constitute this tragedy, and which are almost totally deprived of what we now designate by the name of action.

THE STORY OF "ALCESTE."

Admète, King of Phérès in Thessalia, was at the point of death; when Apollo, who, exiled from heaven by the anger of Jupiter, had been, during the time of his disgrace, a shepherd to Admète, deceives the Fates and hides the young king from their fury. The goddesses, however, only consent to spare the life of Admète on condition of another victim being delivered to them; and it is therefore requisite that someone should be found to offer themselves to die in his place. No one having come forward for this purpose, the Queen offers herself for death, in place of her husband. From a rather lively debate which takes place upon this subject from the very opening of the piece, between Apollo and Orcus (the Genius of Death) it appears that the devotion of the Queen is already known and accepted by Admète himself. He loves

Alceste with passion, but he loves his own life still more; and, though with regret, he allows himself to be saved at this extreme cost.

Profound grief of all the characters; general mourning; heartrending cries of the children of Alceste; lamentations of the people; terror and despair of the young Queen, who, though she has offered herself, trembles before the accomplishment of her sacrifice. Touching scene, in which the dying Queen conjures Admète, who is in tears, to remain faithful to her, and not to lead another spouse to the altar of Hymen. Admète pledges himself; and the Queen, consoled, expires in his arms. They prepare the funeral ceremony, bringing the ornaments and gifts, which have to be placed with Alceste in the tomb. It is then that the old man, Phérès, appears. He is the father of Admète; and the scene which now takes place, though abominable according to our ideas and manners, is none the less evidently sublime. I leave to the translator the responsibility of his translation.

DIALOGUE BETWEEN PHÉRÈS AND ADMÈTE.

Phérès:

"I sympathise with your trouble, my son. The loss which you have sustained is considerable, we must agree. You lose an accomplished spouse; but, however overwhelming may be the weight of your misfortune, you must bear it. Receive from my hand these precious vestments, in order to place them in the tomb. We could not too greatly honour a spouse who has been willing to immolate herself for her husband. It is to her that I owe the happiness of a son's preservation. She could not suffer that a father, in despair, should spend his aged days in mourning."

* * * * * *

Admète:

"I have not called you to these obsequies; and, not to conceal anything from you, your presence here is not at all agreeable to me. Take those vestments away; they shall never be placed upon the body of Alceste. I shall be able to arrange for her to do without your gifts, in the tomb. You saw me on the point of dying. What did you do then? Does it become you, now, to shed tears? After having fled from the danger which threatened me; after having allowed Alceste to die in the flower of her age; whilst you are bent beneath the weight of years? No, I am no longer your son; and do not recognise you for my father."

* * * * * *

"You must be the most unworthy of men; for, though arrived at the end of your career, you had neither the will nor the courage to die for your son, and were even not ashamed to allow that duty to be fulfilled by another."

* * * * * *

Phérès:

"My son! to whom is this haughty speech addressed? Do you think you are speaking to some slave of Lydia, or Phrygia? When has either nature or Greece imposed upon fathers the law of dying for their children? You accuse me of unworthiness; but, yourself unworthy, you have not blushed to employ all your efforts to prolong your days beyond the fatal term, by sacrificing your own spouse. A fine artifice it is indeed! to elude death by persuading one's wife that she has to die for her husband!"

* * * * * *

Then follows a rapid, precipitate dialogue; in which the interlocutors overwhelm each other with atrocious sayings, such as the following:

Admète:

"Old age has lost all shame!"

Phérès:

"Go and marry several wives: that is the way to live long."

* * * * * *

Admète:

Go! You, and your unworthy wife, go and drag out a miserable old age, without children, although I am still living; that is the price of your cowardice. I wish for nothing in common with you, not even a dwelling place; and why can I not with decency forbid you your palace? I should not blush to do it, even in public."

REFLECTIONS ON THE DIALOGUE.

One cannot read this without shuddering. Shakespeare has gone no farther. These two poets seem to have been familiar with each unexplored crevice of the human heart; those dark caverns of which ordinary minds do not dare to sound the forbidding depths; into which the burning glance of genius can alone penetrate without fear, and whence it emerges, dragging out and exposing to the light of day, monsters whose hideous natures surpass belief. They surpass belief, but are only too real; for where are the men who would refuse the devotion of even the most beloved wife in order to sacrifice herself to preserve their life? They exist, no doubt; but they are certainly as rare as are also the women who are capable of such an act of devotion. Each one of us may say: "I think that I belong to them." But the poet-philosopher will answer us: "Alas! it may be you deceive yourselves; and, after all, would rather sigh than die."

Phérès is right: *everyone in this world is for himself. To you, the light of day is sweet and precious. Think you that to me it is so any less?* Molière, twenty centuries later, makes one of his most honest characters say when speaking of his body:

"A mere rag, if you will; but a rag which is very dear to me." And La Fontaine has said the very same thing as the Admète of Euripides; even almost in the very same terms:

Le plus semblable aux morts meurt le plus à regret.

THE STORY OF "ALCESTE" RESUMED.

In the midst of these terrible scenes, in which the young king shows himself exasperated by grief, even to the point of parricidal impiety, a stranger appears.

"Oh! ye inhabitants of Phérès," says he, "shall I find Admète in this palace?"

It is Hercules—this knight-errant of antiquity. He comes in obedience to an order of Eurystée, King of Tyrinthe; in order to take from Diomède, son of Mars, the anthropophagous horses, which Diomède alone has been hitherto able to subdue. Passing Phérès, in the course of fulfilling this dangerous mission, the valiant son of Alcmène wishes to see his friend. Admète advances; inviting him to enter his palace. But the air of consternation shown by the young king astonishes Hercules; and stops him while still upon the hospitable threshold.

"What misfortune has befallen you? Have you lost your father?"—"No."—"Your son?"—"No."—"Alceste? I know that she has engaged to die for you."

Admète again dissimulates; assuring Hercules that the woman who is being mourned is a stranger brought up in the palace. He fears that, should he confess the truth, his friend will refuse the hospitality which is offered him in the desolate household—a refusal which could only be counted as a new misfortune. At last, Hercules enters; allowing himself to be conducted to the allotted apartment, where the slaves prepare for him a sumptuous feast. And the King adds these touching words:

"Shut the middle vestibule. It would be indecent to trouble a feast with cries and tears. It must be concealed from the eyes and ears of our guest that we are engaged in funeral preparatives."

Hercules, allowing himself to become partly assured, takes his place at table; crowns himself with myrtle, eats, drinks and, at last, being somewhat excited, causes the palace to re-echo with his songs. This goes on until the moment when, struck by the stupor of the slaves who are serving him, he questions them; finally learning the truth.

"Alceste dead! Ye gods! And how can you, in this situation, have had regard to hospitality?" (Shakespeare also says, by Cassius to Brutus, whom he has just insulted: "Portia is dead; and you have not killed me!")[2]

---

[2] The above is the literal translation of the text of Berlioz. The original passage in Shakespeare's "Julius Cæsar," to which he refers, runs thus:

> BRUTUS.— . . . . Portia is dead.
> CASSIUS.—Ha! Portia!
> BRUTUS.—She is dead.
> CASSIUS.—How 'scaped I killing, when I cross'd you so?

"ALCESTE" (ORIGINAL).

Hercules:

"Alceste no more! Yet, wretched man, I have allowed my joy to resound in feasting, have crowned my head with flowers in the house of a despairing friend. But it is you who are guilty of this crime. Why did you not reveal to me this fatal mystery? Where is the tomb? Speak! Which is the road for me to follow?

The Officer:

"That which leads to Larisse. On issuing from the faubourg, the tomb will present itself at once to your view."

Hercules then goes to the tomb; places himself in ambuscade; and, pouncing upon Orcus at the moment when he comes to drink the blood of his victims, compels him, notwithstanding all efforts, to give up Alceste, living. Returning with her to the palace, Hercules presents her, veiled, to Admète.

"You see this woman," says Hercules to Admète, "I confide her to your care; and expect from your friendship that you will guard her until, after having killed Diomède and carried off his coursers, I return triumphant."

Admète supplicates him not to exact such a service; as the very sight of a woman, seeming to recall Alceste to his mind, would tear his heart.

The persistence of Hercules becomes such that Admète dares not refuse his request, and he accordingly tenders his hand to the veiled woman; upon which Hercules, being satisfied, at once lifts the veil which hides the stranger's features; and Admète, dismayed, recognises Alceste. But why does she remain both motionless and silent? Dedicated to the infernal divinities, she must be purified; and it is only in three days that she can be completely restored to the tenderness of her happy spouse. Public rejoicings are ordered; Hercules starts upon his perilous voyage; and the tragedy concludes with the following "morality" of the chorus:

"What wonderful means the gods employ to compass the ends which they propose! By their secret power the great events which they control bloom before the astonished gaze of mortals. Such is the prodigy we celebrate, with admiration and with joy."

Our hack dramatic-writers are strong in a way quite different from that of Euripides; and it may be seen, from the above rapid analysis of the Greek poem, that they have good reason to say:

It has no plot.

THE "ALCESTE" OF QUINAULT.

Let us now see what this narrative of conjugal devotion has become in the hands of Quinault; who, also, was admittedly not much of a play-fabricator.

His opera opens with a prologue; in common with the majority of works composed at that time for the

"ALCESTE" (QUINAULT).

Royal Academy of Music. In this prologue, the nymphs of the Seine, of the Marne, and of the Tuileries express their desire to see the King return; and address their reproaches to Glory for detaining him so long.

> Tout languit avec moi dans ces lieux pleins d'appas.
> Le héros que j'attends ne reviendra-t-il pas?
>   Serai-je toujours languissante
>   Dans une si cruelle attente?[3]

When the nymphs of the Seine, the Marne and the Tuileries; the Pleasures and Glory; together with the French naïdes and hamadryads think they have sung enough nonsense, the piece begins.

Alceste has just espoused Admète; rejecting the two suitors for her hand, Hercules and Lycomède, brother of Thétis and King of the island of Scyros. Under pretext of inviting her to a nautical display, Lycomède induces Alceste to visit one of his ships. But, scarcely has the princess, who has imprudently come without her husband, arrived on board, than the perfidious Lycomède lifts anchor; and, assisted by his sister, Thétis, who sends him favourable winds, he conducts Alceste to Scyros. The rape is consummated. The two rivals of Lycomède now starting in his pursuit, Hercules and Admète arrive at Scyros. They besiege the town, force its gates and put everything to fire and sword; singing:

---

[3] All unites with me in sadness in this delightful place. Will not the hero I expect soon return? Or shall I still be left to suffer this cruel delay?

> Donnons, donnons, de toutes parts
> Que chacun à l'envi combatte
> Que l'on abatte
> Les tours et les remparts.[4]

Alceste is recovered; and probably Lycomède is killed, since we do not hear any more of him. But, in course of the fight, Admète has become seriously wounded; and will surely die unless someone volunteers to die in his stead.

The scene represents a grand monument erected by the arts; and, in the middle, there appears an empty altar, destined to perpetuate the memory of the heroic person who may sacrifice himself for Admète. No one appearing, Alceste dedicates herself; the altar opens, she is seen to pierce her breast; and, now that she has descended to the bourne of the shades, there is general desolation.

Hercules, who was upon the point of starting off to conquer some tyrant, now alters his mind; addressing Admète in the following singular fashion:

> J'aime Alceste; il est temps de ne m'en plus defendre
> Elle meurt; ton amour n'a plus rien à prétendre.
> Admète, cède-moi, la beauté que tu perds;
> Au palais de Pluton j'entreprends de descendre:
> J'irai jusqu'au fonds des enfers
> Forcer la mort à me la rendre.[5]

---

[4] Strike on every side and let each one strive to excel in the fight; every tower and rampart being razed to the ground.

[5] I love Alceste; from now I may declare it, for, as she dies, your love is at an end. Admète confer upon me the beauty you are losing, and I undertake to descend to the palace of Pluto. I shall go to the very bottom of hell, and force death to give her back to me.

Admète consents to this strange transaction, and replies to Hercules:

> Qu'elle vive pour vous avec tous ses appas,
> Admète est trop heureux pourvu qu'Alceste vive.[6]

The great Alcide now arrives at the banks of the Styx. He there finds Charon; pushing back, by means of great blows from his oar, the miserable shades who have not the means of paying their passage.

> A Shade (who has no money).—Hélas! Caron, hélas! hélas!
> Caron.—
> Crie hélas! tant que tu voudras,
> Rien pour rien en tous lieux est une loi suivie;
> Les mains vides sont sans appas,
> Et ce n'est point assez de payer dans la vie,
> Il faut encor payer au delà du trépas.[7]

Hercules rushes into the boat, which creaks under his weight and lets in water at several places. He succeeds in getting to the other bank, however; and, arrived at the palace of Pluton, Alecton gives the alarm, upon which Pluton, being furious, cries out:

> Qu'on arrête ce téméraire;
> Armez-vous, amis, armez-vous
> Qu'on déchaîne Cerbère,
> Courez tous, Courez tous.[8]

We hear the bark of Cerberus.

---

[6] She may live for you in all the fullness of her grace. Admète is only too happy if Alceste does but live.

[7] Cry, alas, as much as you please. Nothing for nothing is the universal law. Empty hands have no attraction, and paying does not end with life: you must pay on the other side of the grave, as well.

[8] Stop that rash fool! Arm yourselves; unchain Cerberus; hasten all!

But Proserpine is moved by the love which Alcide shows for Alceste; and persuades Pluton to give her up to him.

> Il faut que l'amour extrême
> Soit plus fort
> Que la mort.[9]

Alceste, now returned to earth, weeps upon learning that she has become the property of her liberator; and Admète, for his part, is the reverse of gay. There is a general sadness which Hercules perceives:

> Vous détournez les yeux! je vous trouve insensible!
> ALCESTE.—
> > Je fais ce qui m'est possible
> > Pour ne regarder que vous.[10]

This does not suit Hercules; but as, after all, this demi-god is a brave fellow, he endeavours to conquer himself; and, giving back Alceste to her husband, he sings:

> Non, vous ne devez pas croire
> Qu'un vainqueur de tyrans soit tyran à son tour.
> Sur l'enfer, sur la mort j'emporte la victoire;
> Il ne manque plus à ma gloire
> Que de triompher de l'Amour.[11]

And that is why this curious opera is called "Alceste,

---

[9] Extreme love must be stronger than death.

[10] You turn away your glance, I find you cold. (Alceste) I do my best only to look at you.

[11] No, you must not think that a conqueror of tyrants can be a conqueror in his turn. I have triumphed over death and hell; my glory now only requires that I should triumph over love.

or the Triumph of Alcide." Besides those which I have mentioned there are, in this lyric tragedy, many other characters; as, for example, a little oddity of fifteen years of age, one of Alceste's waiting-women, who is loved by both Lycas and Straton, confidants of Hercules and Lycomède, and who takes upon herself to lecture them, whenever they press her to make a choice, something in the following way:

> Je n'ai point de choix à faire :
> Parlons d'aimer et de plaire,
> Et vivons toujours en paix,
> L'hymen détruit la tendresse,
> Il rend l'amour sans attraits :
> Voulez-vous aimez sans cesse?
> Amants, n'épousez jamais.[12]

We must admit that Boileau was not far out in castigating these poetic concoctions:

> Et tous ces lieux communs de morale lubrique
> Que Lulli réchauffa des sons de sa musique.[1]

only, that instead of saying that Lulli had *warmed* it with the strains of his music he ought to have said *chilled*; for it would be impossible to imagine anything more icy, languid, flat and miserable than this setting; which is both out of date and childish.

---

[12] I have no choice to make. Let us only speak of loving and pleasing, and of living always at peace. Marriage puts an end to all tenderness and takes all the attraction away from love. If you want to love for ever, lovers, never marry.

[1] And all the lewdness that Lulli set off (warmed) with the sounds of his music.

That excellent singer, Alizard, has several times performed, at concerts and with some success, the scene of Caron with the shades.

The rhythm gives to this piece a certain compactness which pleases the public, and which they laughingly applaud; without knowing, precisely, whether they are laughing at the words or the music. The expression of the vocal part is truthful, and the theme:

> Il faut passer tôt ou tard
> Il faut passer dans ma barque.[2]

corresponds remarkably well with a partly grotesque version of the character of Caron, such as that of Quinault.

THE SCORE OF LULLI.

If it is now desired to form a fairly accurate idea of the musical style of Lulli, this may be easily done by listening, at the Théâtre-Français, to the pieces which he has written for the comedies of Molière; for the music of "Alceste" has precisely the colour, the tone and general bearing of that of the "Bourgeois Gentilhomme."

His ideas were very spare; besides which he applied, to all subjects, the only procedure in composition which he knew anything about. That was obliged to be the case with all musicians during an early stage

---

[2] Sooner or later all must pass over in my boat.

of the art; and thus it happens that Palestrina, writing in a style essentially different, composed table-songs just like his masses; and that so many other composers wrote masses just like their table-songs.

There is a widespread opinion which attributes the monotony of the works of ancient composers to the slender resources which were at their disposition. It is customary to say:

"The instruments which we employ were not then invented."

That is an evident mistake. Palestrina wrote only for voices; and the singers of his period were probably fully capable of executing other things besides counterpoint in five or six parts. As to instrumentalists, although, at the time of Lulli they were untrained and of incontestable inferiority compared with ours, a modern composer of talent could easily produce excellent effects, even with the moderate executants that Lulli had at his command. We must not attribute such great importance to the *material means* of the art of sounds. A sonata of Beethoven, executed upon a spinet, would nevertheless remain a marvel of inspiration; whilst many other works which I might mention, even if played upon the most magnificent Erard or Broadwood piano, would remain mere nonsense and platitude.

The arts, in the early stages of their progress, have not yet learned all the words of their language; and a crowd of prejudices, from which they are very slow to escape, stands materially in the way of acquiring this knowledge. But, let a man of true genius appear; a man possessed of that combination of faculties which necessarily includes, along with the creative power, good sense, in the higher signification of the word. This means that he will have the force, intelligence and courage to despise the judgments of the crowd which are prevalent at those dim periods; and that, in spite of all obstacles, he will be able to impart, to the special art to which he is devoted, a sudden forward movement; even if, single-handed, he is unable to effect its complete emancipation. Such a man was Gluck, whose great work we are now about to study.

GLUCK'S EARLY EXPERIENCES.

We have seen what the "Alceste" of Eurypides became in the hands of Quinault with the strange kind of poetry—

> That Lulli did but *chill* with paltry sounds of music.[3]

Later on, there came a man who was not, like the Florentine musician,

> Esquire,
> Councillor,
> Royal secretary, etc.

nor even superintendent of music to any royal personage; but who had a powerful intelligence, a warm

---

[3] Que Lulli *refroidit* des sons de sa musique (Berlioz).

heart full of love for the beautiful and a bold spirit; in short, it was Gluck who came, and who, casting his eyes upon the "Alceste" of Eurypides, chose it for the text of an opera. His idea was to write this work in such a style that it should form the point of departure for a complete revolution in dramatic music. Gluck was then living in Vienna, having previously made a long stay in Italy; and it was during that period that he had conceived so profound a contempt for the system of musical composition then in use for the theatre. He found that it disagreed with common sense, and was in opposition to the most noble instincts of the human heart; for, according to it, an opera became generally a mere pretext for singers to appear upon the stage and

play the larynx

precisely in the same manner as is customary with the virtuoso; who appears upon a concert-platform, say, to play the clarinet or oboe.

He saw that musical art possessed a power which was great in a far different sense from that of merely tickling the ear with agreeable vocalisations; and he asked himself why this power of expression, which, in melody, harmony and instrumentation could not be mistaken, should not be employed to produce works reasonable, moving and worthy of exciting the interest of an audience composed of serious and cultured people. Without excluding sensation, he desired that it should be subordinate to sentiment; and without considering poetry the principal object of the opera, his idea was that it should be so united to the music as to form one with it; in order that, from this union, a force of expression might result, far greater than that obtainable from either art when employed separately. An Italian poet, who was then living at Vienna, and with whom Gluck had frequent interviews on this subject, entered with warmth and conviction into his views; helping him to form a plan for this indispensable reform, and becoming, as we shall see, his intelligent collaborator.

GLUCK AND HIS ITALIAN SCORES.

We must not imagine, however, that Gluck decided suddenly to introduce expressive and dramatic music upon the stage, merely in the case of "Alceste." "Orfeo," which preceded "Alceste," alone proves the contrary. He had, in fact, experimented upon this new departure for a long time. He was naturally impelled in this direction, and already, in many portions of his Italian scores, written in Italy and for Italians, he had ventured to introduce numbers in a style most severe, expressive and nobly beautiful. A proof that they merit this praise lies in the fact that, at a later date, he himself found them worthy of a place in his most illustrious French scores; for which people incorrectly think that they were written, such is the care and sagacity with which they have been adapted to new situations.

The air of Telemaco:

> Umbra mesta del padre,

in the Italian opera of the same name, was transformed into the duet, now so famous, in "Armide":

> Esprits de haine et de rage.[4]

We may also quote, among the numbers of this Italian score, which he has, so to speak, despoiled for the benefit of his French operas, an air of Ulysse which is used as the subject of the instrumental introduction of the overture to "Iphigenia in Aulide." Another air of Telemaco appears again, almost completely, as that of Oreste in "Iphigenia in Tauride"; entitled:

> Dieux qui me poursuivez;[5]

the entire scene of Circé, evoking the infernal spirits, in order that they may change the companions of Ulysse into beasts, has become that of "Hatred" in "Armide"; the great air of Circé has been converted, by some development of its orchestration, into the air in A, of the fourth act of "Iphigenia in Tauride":

> Je t'implore et je tremble;[6]

and, finally, the overture, which he has merely enriched by an episodial theme, has been used again as overture

---

[4] Spirits of hatred and rage.
[5] Ye gods who pursue me.
[6] I implore you and I tremble.

to the opera of "Armide." We may even regret his not having completed the pillage of "Telemaco" by employing somewhere the adorable air of the nymph Asteria:

> Ah! l'ho presente ognor;

which is a marvel. The regrets of a despised love are so beautifully expressed in this elegy that, never since that time, in the works of any master, or even in those of Gluck himself, has so beautiful a musical form been given to them, or such melodiously sorrowful accents been used to voice the feelings of a broken heart.

Finally in order to terminate the list of Gluck's borrowings from his Italian scores, from which we derive such evident proof of his having written *dramatic* music long before the production of "Alceste," let us quote the immortal air:

> O malheureuse Iphigénie

from "Iphigenia in Tauride," which was taken in its entirety from his Italian opera, "Tito"; besides the charming chorus in the French opera of "Alceste":

> Parez vos fronts de fleurs nouvelles;[7]

and the final chorus of "Iphigenia in Tauride":

> Les dieux longtemps en courroux,[8]

---

[7] Deck your brows with fresh-culled flowers.
[8] The gods so long in anger.

both of which were taken from the score of "Elena-e Paride."

CALSABIGI'S LIBRETTO OF "ALCESTE."

The choice of a subject to be treated in a new opera having thus fallen upon the "Alceste" of Euripides, Calsabigi, then poet at the court of Marie-Therèse, and who understood well the genius and intentions of Gluck, set himself to work. He prudently eliminated from the Greek poem all that we nowadays regard as defects, and was successful in bringing to the front new situations highly dramatic and, it must be admitted, conspicuously favourable to the main developments of an opera; though I consider that he was wrong in suppressing the character of Hercules, which it would have been possible to turn to such good account. At the start of the action in his poem the Thessalian people are assembled before the palace of Phérès, waiting for news of the health of Admète who is grievously ill. A herald announces to the anxious crowd that the King is approaching his last moments. The Queen appears, followed by her children, and invites the people to proceed with her to the temple of Apollo; there to invoke the assistance of that god in favour of Admète.

The scene changes, and the religious ceremony commences in the temple. The priest consults the entrails of the victims; and, seized with terror, he announces that the god is about to speak. The people bow low and, in the midst of a solemn silence, the voice of the oracle pronounces these words:

> Il re morrà s'altro per lui non more,
>
> Le roi doit mourir aujourd'hui,
> Si quelque autre au trépas ne se livre pour lui.[9]

The priest then asks the terrified crowd:

> Which of you is willing to offer himself for death? No one answers! Then your king must die.

The crowd tumultuously disperses, leaving the Queen half fainting at the foot of the altar. But Admète will not die; for Alceste, with a sublime impulse of heroic tenderness, approaches the statue of Apollo, and solemnly swears to give her life for her husband. The priest returns and announces to Alceste that her sacrifice is accepted; and that, at the close of the day, the ministers of the god of the dead will come and wait for her at the gates of hell. This act is full of movement, and excites a lively emotion.

In the second act the whole town of Phérès is intoxicated with joy; Admète is restored to health and we see him, all smiles, receiving the felicitations of his friends. But Alceste does not appear, and the King is uneasy on account of her absence. They tell him she is at the temple, whither she has gone to give thanks to the gods for the restoration of the King. Alceste returns; and, notwithstanding all her efforts, she cannot join in the public rejoicings, but gives way to pain-

---

[9] The king dies to-day unless another offers to take his place.

ful signs of grief. Admète first begs her, and at last orders her to make known to him the cause of her tears; upon which the unfortunate woman avows the truth. Thereupon follows the despair of the King, who refuses to allow the frightful immolation to take place; and swears that, if Alceste persists in her design, it will not save him, as in that case, he will prefer to die.

However, the hour approaches; and Alceste, having succeeded in eluding the King's attention, has betaken herself to the entrance of Tartarus.

"What will you?" is the cry which reaches her, and which proceeds from invisible voices. "The moment is not yet come. Wait until the day shall have given place to darkness." At these strange and lugubrious accents, as well as at the sombre rays of light which escape from the infernal cave, Alceste feels her reason abandon her. She runs distracted round the altar of death; staggering, half mad with terror, though still remaining firm in her purpose. Admète, who has been pursuing her, now arrives; and renews his supplications in order to dissuade her from her purpose. But, during this heartrending debate, the hour has drawn near; and an infernal divinity, issuing from the abyss, descends upon the altar of death; from the summit of which it calls upon the Queen to keep her promise.

From the bank of the Styx, Caron, the ferryman of the dead, calls Alceste by a summons thrice repeated, in raw and cavernous tones, issuing from his trumpet of sea-shell. The god, however, allows Alceste a further refuge from her terrible resolution, being willing to release her from her vow; and offering her the alternative that, if she revokes it, Admète dies upon the instant.

"Let him live!" she cries "and show me the way to Hell!" At once, and notwithstanding the cries of Admète, demons make their appearance in order to seize the Queen and drag her into Tartarus. In the drama of Calsabigi, Apollo appeared in a cloud, shortly afterwards, and restored the living Alceste to her husband. This conclusion had, at first, been also preserved in the French piece; but, a few years after the first representation Durollet, the author of the translation of Alceste from the Italian, thought it better to make Hercules suddenly intervene; and it is he now who descends into hell to restore Alceste. Apollo appears, notwithstanding; but only to congratulate the hero upon his good action and to assure him that a place is already assigned for him among the gods.

It will be seen that Calsabigi complied with the exigencies of modern taste and manners in the arrangement of his drama; as there is a plot, besides all the necessary action and surprises. Admète, far from accepting the devotion of the Queen, is in despair in being apprised of it. The temple-scene, which is not found, and could not be found in Eurypides, is one of striking majesty. The character of Alceste, whose heart is noble though not intrepid, and who trembles before the accomplishment of a vow which she nevertheless fulfils, is well sustained. The public rejoicings after the restoration of the King to health, form a most powerful contrast with the grief of the Queen, unable to restrain her tears, and yet obliged to be present.

But, in spite of all that Gluck says in his dedicatory epistle to the Archduke Leopold, grand-duke of Tuscany, the poem of Alceste contains little variety. The accents of pain, dismay and despair succeed one another continually, with the result that the public become speedily fatigued. This accounts for the reproaches cast upon Gluck's music, both at Vienna and Paris—reproaches which should really be applied only to the libretto. As to the music, on the contrary, one cannot sufficiently admire the richness of ideas, the constant inspiration and the vehemence of accent with which Gluck, from one end to the other of his score, was enabled to combat, as far as possible, this unfortunate monotony.

Over twenty years ago we already made an examination in detail of Gluck's system, and of the explanation which he gives of it in the dedicatory epistle, forming a preface, to the Italian "Alceste." We now ask permission to return to this, and to add to it some new observations.

GLUCK'S ACCOUNT OF HIS OWN SYSTEM.

"When I undertook to set the opera of 'Alceste' to music I proposed to myself to avoid all the abuses that the mistaken vanity of singers and the excessive complaisance of composers had introduced into Italian opera, and which had converted the most stately and beautiful of all spectacles into one of the most tiresome and ridiculous. I sought to confine the music to its true function, that of assisting the poetry, by strengthening both the expression of the sentiments and the interest of the situations; and this without either interrupting the action or chilling it by the introduction of superfluous ornaments. I thought that music should add to the poetry precisely what is added to a correct and well conceived drawing, when the vivacity of the colours and the happy harmony of light and shade serve to animate the figures, without changing their outline.

"I have taken particular care not to interrupt an actor, in the warmth of dialogue, in order to make him wait for the end of a ritornello; or, to stop him in the middle of his discourse upon a favourable vowel; either for the purpose of providing a long passage for the display of the agility of his beautiful voice, or, in order that he should wait for the orchestra to give him time to take breath for a cadence. I have not thought it necessary to pass rapidly over the second part of an air, although it might be one of the most passionate and important; and finish the air, notwithstanding that there is no conclusion in the sense, merely to give the singer an opportunity of showing his capability, by capriciously rendering a passage in different ways. In short, I have tried to banish all these abuses, against which good sense and reason have protested so long in vain.

"I have imagined that the overture should warn the spectators of the character of the action to be submitted to them, as well as indicate its subject; that the instruments should only be requisitioned in proportion to the degree of interest or passion; and that it was necessary to avoid, in the dialogue, too violent a distinction between the air and the recitative; to secure that the period should not be marked off abruptly, in interruption of the sense; and that the movement and the warmth of the scene should not be inappropriately intruded upon. My belief has also been that the work should, above all things, aim at a beautiful simplicity; and I have thus avoided all parade of difficulties, at the expense of clearness. I have not attached the least value to the discovery of a novelty, unless naturally suggested by the situation and wedded to its expression. Finally, there is no rule which I have not felt I ought willingly to sacrifice in favour of effect."

CRITICAL EXAMINATION OF GLUCK'S ACCOUNT.

This profession of faith seems to us, on the whole, admirable in point of frankness and good sense. The points of doctrine which form the basis of it and which, for some years, have been so basely and ridiculously abused, are founded upon just reasonings and a profound sentiment for true dramatic music. With the exception of a few which we shall shortly indicate, these principles are of such excellence that they have been followed in great part by the majority of good composers of all nations. But Gluck, in promulgating this theory, the necessity of which was dictated by even the faintest sentiment of art, or by ordinary common sense, has, in some instances, exaggerated its results. It would be difficult to mistake this after an impartial examination; and he has not even in his own works applied the theory he proposes, with an altogether rigorous exactitude. Thus, in the Italian "Alceste," we find recitatives accompanied only by figured bass, and probably by chords of the cembalo (clavichord), as was then the custom in Italian theatres. It results that, from this kind of accompaniment and this sort of vocal recitation, a "violent distinction" does arise between the recitative and the air. Several of his airs are preceded by a long instrumental solo; thus compelling the singer to keep silence and "wait for the end of the ritornello." Moreover, he frequently employs a form of air which is forbidden by his own theory of dramatic music. I allude to airs with repeats and the repeated parts in which are sung twice; without these repetitions being in any way justified, but appearing precisely as if the public had demanded an encore. Such is the air of Alceste:

> Je n'ai jamais chéri la vie
> Que pour te prouver mon amour
> Ah ! pour te conserver le jour
> Qu'elle me soit cent fois ravie ![10]

---

[10] I have never valued life, except to prove to you my love To preserve your days let it be taken from me a hundred times.

Now, when the melody has arrived at the cadence on the dominant, why should he have recommenced, without the slightest change, either in the vocal part or in the orchestra, with:

Je n'ai jamais chéri la vie, etc.?

Assuredly, dramatic sense is shocked by this proceeding; and, if anyone should have abstained from this offence against nature and similitude, it was Gluck. Notwithstanding that, he has committed it in nearly all his works. No examples of it are to be found in modern music; from which it follows that Gluck's successors have been more severe upon the point than he was himself.

When he says that the music of a lyric drama is designed only to add to the poetry what colour adds to a drawing, I consider that he is essentially in error. It seems to me that the task of an opera composer is of quite another importance. His work contains both the design and the colour; and, if we are to retain Gluck's comparison, we should say that the words are the *subject* of the picture—scarcely anything more. Expression is not the only object of dramatic music; and it would be both clumsy and pedantic to disdain the purely sensual pleasure which we find in certain effects of melody, harmony, rhythm or instrumentation; independently of any reference they may have to the sentiments and passions of the drama.

But, even in the case of wishing to deprive the listener of this source of enjoyment, and to forbid him to revive his attention by diverting it for a moment from its principal object, there would still be a great number of cases in which the composer is called upon to sustain the entire interest of a lyric work. In character-dances, for example, during dumb-show, in marches; in short—everywhere where instrumental music is used alone, and without words, what becomes of the importance of the poet? The music must there, perforce, include both design and colour.

If we except a few of those brilliant orchestral sonatas, in which the genius of Rossini found such graceful play, it is certain that, thirty years ago, the majority of instrumental compilations which the Italians honoured with the name of "overture" were nothing but grotesque nonsense. But, how very much more absurd they must have been a hundred years ago; when their example had so much influence on Gluck (who, by the way, we may as well admit was by no means as great a musician in the ordinary, as in the scenic, sense) that he was not afraid to allow the incredible nonsense which he calls "Overture to Orphée" to issue from his pen. He did better for "Alceste," and especially for "Iphigenia in Aulide." His theory of expressive overtures gave the impulse; and this, later on, produced such symphonic masterpieces that, notwithstanding the fall or the profound neglect of the works for which they were written, these overtures have remained; standing, like superb peristyles, as all that remains of temples which have fallen into decay. However, in this also, through the exaggeration of a correct idea, Gluck has fallen into error; not, this time, in the direction of minimising the power of music, but in that of attributing to it, on the contrary, a power which it will never possess. I mean when he says that the overture should indicate the *subject* of the piece. Musical expression does not go so far as that. It may reproduce joy or grief, gravity or cheerfulness; it may set up a salient difference between the joy of a pastoral people and that of a warlike nation; or, between the grief of a Queen and the chagrin of a simple village girl; or, between a serious and calm meditation and the ardent reverie which precedes an outburst of passion. Then, borrowing from different nations their own peculiar musical style, it is evident that it may also distinguish between the serenade of a brigand of Aprutium and that of a Scotch or Tyrolean chasseur; or, that it may easily mark a distinction between the nocturnal tread of a crowd of pilgrims, of mystic habits, and the march of a troop of cattle-dealers coming home from a fair. It may also express the natural opposition between extreme brutality, triviality and the grotesque, on the one hand; and angelic purity, nobleness and sincerity on the other.

But, if music endeavours to go beyond this immense circle, it must of necessity have recourse to words; either sung, recited or merely read, in order to fill up the gaps which its means of expression unavoidably leave, in a work which appeals both to the mind and to the imagination. Thus, the overture to "Alceste" will announce scenes of desolation and tenderness; but it will be unable to reveal either the object of the tenderness or the cause of the desolation. It can never inform the spectator that the husband of Alceste is a King of Thessalia, condemned by the gods to lose his life unless someone volunteers to die in his place: that, however, is the *subject* of the piece. Some readers may be astonished to find the author of this article imbued by such principles; thanks to certain people who have either believed, or pretended to believe that, in his opinions about musical expression, he was as far ahead of the truth as he was behind it; and who have, consequently, generously presented him with their quota of ridicule. Let this be said, however, merely in passing; and without rancour.

The third proposition in Gluck's theory, the application of which I shall permit myself to contest, is that by which he disclaims having attached any value to the "discovery of a novelty." They had already, in his time, spoiled much music paper; and any musical discovery, even though only indirectly allied to scenic expression, was not to be despised.

All his other principles are, I believe, however, well able to withstand all combat; and even the last can stand its ground, though it expresses a contempt for rule, which many professors will be sure to find blasphemous or impious. Gluck, although I repeat that he was not a musician of a force equal to that of some of his successors, was amply competent to assume the right of answering his critics in the same way as Beethoven did on one occasion:

"Who forbids that harmony?"
"Fux, Albrechtsberger and twenty other theorists."
"Well, I permit it."

or of giving them the same laconic reply as that which proceeded from one of our greatest poets when reading a work of his composition before the committee of the Théâtre Français. One of the members of the Areopagus interrupted him, timidly, in the middle of his lecture.

"What is it, sir?" asked the poet, with severe calm.
"Only that it seems to me that—er——er—that is, I find it er——"
"What, then, sir?"
"That such an expression is not strictly French!"
"It *will* be so, sir!"

The self-confidence of such an assurance is even more becoming in the musician than in the poet; for it is more permissible to believe in the proximate acceptance of his neologisms, his language being not one of convention.

ANALYSIS OF GLUCK'S "ALCESTE."

We are now in possession of Gluck's theories on the subject of dramatic music; and, certainly, "Alceste" is one of his most magnificent applications of them;

the French score being so in a highly marked degree. During the years which intervened between the composition of this work at Vienna and its representation at Paris, the genius of the composer seems to have become increased and consolidated. The opposition offered him by the Italians appears to have doubled his strength and to have given more penetration to his mind. The result is shown in the admirable transformation of the Italian "Alceste"; several numbers of which have been integrally preserved (they are so lovely that we lose sight of any possible improvement), and of which other numbers (with one exception which we shall refer to) have been appreciably beautified in being introduced to our stage and brought into union with our tongue. The melodic outline of the latter has been generally rendered more spacious and more defined; certain accents have become more penetrating; and the instrumentation has been enriched; assuming at the same time a more ingenious design. Furthermore, a certain number of new pieces, airs, choruses and recitatives, have been added to the score; of which the composer seems to have kneaded the musical element, as the clay-modeller does his material in making a statue.

When I read again my former criticism of the score of "Alceste," I find some observations which no longer appear to me to be just. I had, however, been much struck by all the beauties which it contains, and I shall certainly never forget the impression made upon me at the general rehearsal which I attended; that being the occasion of the resumption of the principal part by Madame Blanchu, in 1825. But I felt myself so passionately in favour of this work that I was haunted by the very fear of falling into a blind fanaticism; and from this I took refuge in blaming certain things which, in reality, I admired. I have no longer that fear; being now quite sure that my admiration is not a blind one, and that there is no need to allow misplaced scruples to attenuate its expression.

The overture, without being very rich in ideas, contains several pathetic and touching accents. A sombre colour predominates; and, although the instrumentation has neither the violence nor the brilliancy of that of our time, it is fuller and stronger, nevertheless, than that of the remaining overtures of Gluck. The trombones figure in it from the beginning; but neither trumpets nor kettledrums make any appearance. In connection with this subject it has to be remarked that, by a most exceptional singularity, there is not a note either for trumpets or kettledrums throughout the entire opera; with the single exception of the two trumpets which appear upon the scene at the moment when the herald desires to speak to the people.

Let us add, in order to put an end to certain popular misconceptions, that Gluck, in his score, employed, in addition to flutes and oboes—clarinets, bassoons, horns and trombones. In the Italian "Alceste" he frequently has recourse to cors anglais; but this instrument, not being known in France at the time of his arrival, he everywhere very skilfully replaced it, in the French "Alceste," by clarinets. Nor does the piccolo at all figure in this work; everything being banished from it which is coarse, noisy or piercing; so that no sonorities have any place in it except such as are either gentle or noble.

The overture of "Alceste," like those of "Iphigenia in Aulide," "Don Giovanni" and "Démophoon," does not conclude before the rise of the curtain; but is joined to the first number of the opera by harmonic sequence, which suspends the cadence indefinitely. I do not quite see, notwithstanding Gluck, Mozart and Vogel all acting in this way, what is the advantage of an incomplete form for overtures. They are better united to the action, it is true; but the listener, disappointed at being deprived of the conclusion of the instrumental preface, experiences a momentary discomfort which is fatal to what has preceded, without being particularly favourable to what follows. The opera gains little by it, while the overture loses much.

At the rise of the curtain the chorus, entering upon a chord which interrupts the harmonic cadence of the orchestra, exclaims:

Dieux, rendez-nous notre roi, notre père ![1]

and thus furnishes us, from the very first bar, with

---

[1] Ye gods, restore to us our king, our father!

material for an observation applicable to the vocal texture of all the other choruses of Gluck.

Everyone knows that the natural classification of human voices is soprano and contralto for women, and tenor and bass for men; and that the female voices are an octave higher than the male, and stand in the same relation to one another; the contralto being a fifth below the soprano as the bass is a fifth below the tenor. They used to pretend at the Opera, even as recently as thirty years ago, that there were no contraltos in France; for which reason French choruses possessed only sopranos, and, in them, the contralto part had to be taken by a voice which was noisy, forced and somewhat rare, called "haute-contre"; which, after all, is nothing but a high tenor.

Gluck, therefore, when he arrived in Paris, was obliged to abandon the excellent choral disposition which he had adopted in Italy and Germany, in order to conform to the French custom. This involved his changing the contralto part to make it suitable for the voice of high tenor. Sixty years afterwards, they discovered that Nature really did produce contralto voices in France—in fact, just the same as everywhere else. Consequently we now possess at the Opera a good supply of these deep female voices, and very few "hautes-contre." They have, therefore, had a good reason for reinstating, nearly everywhere in "Alceste," the natural vocal hierarchy which Gluck had observed in his Italian score. I have said that the restitution of the contralto part was made *nearly* everywhere; because, as a matter of fact, it could not be always done, there being some choruses written for male voices alone, in which the part of "hautes-contre" was still obliged to be left to the first tenors.

The chorus:

> O dieux! qu'allons-nous devenir?[2]

following the announcement of the herald, is full of a noble sadness; the gravity of which increases the effect of the stretta which follows:

> Non, jamais le courroux céleste,

of which the principal melodic designs are also well declaimed and of an accentuation as truthful as that of the best recitative.

It is the same with the dialogued chorus:

> O malheureux Admète;

of which, especially the last phrase:

> Malheureuse patrie!

is of a poignant truthfulness of expression.

In the recitative sung by Alceste at her entrance the entire soul of the young Queen unveils itself in a few bars. The beautiful air:

> Grands dieux, du destin qui m'accable,

is in three movements; one which is slow and in com-

---

[2] O gods! what will become of us?

mon time, another in triple time and the third an agitated allegro. It is in this agitato that the beautiful orchestral accent appears which is afterwards taken up by the voice, with the words:

Quand je vous presse sur mon sein,[3]

and of which a musician said, on one occasion: "It is the heart of the orchestra which is agitated!" This air, in respect of the diction of the words, the sequence of melodic phrases and the art of economising the force of accent until the final explosion, presents difficulties of which the majority of singers have no idea.

The third scene opens in the temple of Apollo. Enter the high-priest and the sacrificers; bringing with them the burning tripods and instruments of sacrifice; whilst, following them, comes Alceste, conducting her children; the courtiers, and then the crowd. Here Gluck gives us local colour, if anyone ever did; for it is literally ancient Greece which he reveals to us, in all its majestic and beautiful simplicity. Listen to the instrumental piece which introduces the cortège; hear (that is, if you do not happen to have some pitiless jabberer sitting next you) that melody, so sweet, veiled and calmly resigned; that pure harmony; and that rhythm, scarcely conscious of the basses, the undulating movements of which are hidden below the rest of the orchestra. Lend your ear to the unaccustomed voice of the flutes in their lower register; to the interweavings of the two

---

[3] When I press you to my breast.

violin parts, taking the melody in dialogue; and say whether there is, in all music, anything more beautiful to be found, in the antique sense of the word, than this religious march. Its instrumentation is simple, but exquisite; and comprises only two wind instruments, in addition to the strings. But there, as in so many other instances in the course of his works, he has hit upon the precise qualities of tone which were necessary. Replace the flutes by two oboes, and everything will be spoiled.

The ceremony commences with a prayer, of which the high-priest alone has pronounced, in a solemn tone, the opening words:

Dieu puissant, écarte du trône

interspersed by three wide chords of C, taken *sotto voce*, afterwards increased in force up to *fortissimo*, by the brass. There could be nothing more imposing than this dialogue between the voice of the priest and the stately harmony of the sacred trumpets. The chorus, after a short silence, resumes the same words in a somewhat animated movement in 6-8 time, both the form and melody of which cause astonishment by their strangeness. The natural expectation would, of course, be that a prayer should be in slow movement; and in any other kind of time than 6-8. How is it that this one, without losing its gravity, allies itself to a kind of tragic agitation, to a strongly marked rhythm and to a bright instrumentation? I am strongly inclined to think that certain religious ceremonies of antiquity, being, as they say, accompanied by saltations or symbolic dances, Gluck, having this idea in mind, wished to impart to his music a character bearing some relation to the custom referred to. The impression produced at the representation by this chorus seems to prove that, notwithstanding the ignorance in which the most able choreographers remain upon the subject of the ritual of ancient sacrifices, the poetical sense of the composer has not misled him.

The *obbligato* recitative of the high priest:

Apollon est sensible à nos gémissements[4]

is evidently the most ingenious and astonishing application of that principle of the composer's system which consists in employing instrumental masses—only in proportion to the prevailing degree of interest and passion. Here, the stringed instruments begin alone in unison; the design thus announced being renewed right up to the end of the scene, with continually increasing energy. At the moment when the prophetic exaltation of the priest begins to manifest itself:

Tout m'annonce du dieu la presence suprême,[5]

the second violins and violas commence a tremulando in arpeggio, which, if it is well executed by pressing hard upon the strings near the bridge, produces an effect resembling the noise of a cataract; and, upon this, a

---

[4] Apollo inclines to hear our cry.
[5] Everything announces to me the supreme presence of the god.

violent stroke by the basses and first violins falls, from time to time. The flutes, oboes and clarinets enter only successively, in the intervals between the exclamations of the inspired pontiff; the horns and the trombones being silent throughout. But, at these words:

> Le saint trépied s'agite
> Tout se remplit d'un juste effroi ![6]

the mass of brass vomits its broadside, so long restrained. The flutes and oboes raise their feminine cries; the shudderings of the violins seem to shake the entire orchestra: "Il va parler." ("He deigns to speak"): then a sudden silence:

> Saisi de crainte et de respect,
> Peuple, observe un profond silence.
> Reine, dépose à son aspect,
> Le vain orgueil de la puissance!
> Tremble ![7]

This last word, pronounced upon a single sustained note, whilst the priest, casting a stray glance upon Alceste, and indicating to her by a gesture the lower steps of the altar where she must bow her royal head, crowns this extraordinary scene in a sublime manner. It is prodigious; being giant's music, of which no one before Gluck ever suspected the possible existence.

After a long general silence, the length of which the composer has marked out with a precision contrary to

---

[6] The sacred tripod moves and all are filled with holy fear.
[7] Seized with fear and respect, people! observe a profound silence. Queen! resign at his aspect all vain pride of power. Tremble.

his usual habit, by making all the voices and instruments count exactly two bars and a half, we hear the voice of the oracle:

> Le roi doit mourir aujourd hui
> Si quelque autre au trépas ne se livre pour lui.[8]

This phrase, delivered almost entirely upon one note, and the solemn trombone chords which accompany it have both been imitated, or rather copied, by Mozart, in "Don Giovanni," for the few words pronounced by the statue of the commander in the cemetery. The chorus, *sotto voce*, which follows is of grand character; and well expresses the stupor and consternation of a people whose love for their King does not quite extend to dying for him. The composer suppressed a chorus in the French opera which, in the Italian, was placed behind the stage; murmuring: "Fuggiamo! fuggiamo!" ("Let us fly! let us fly!") whilst the first chorus, absorbed by its amazement, continued to repeat, without any thought of flight, the words:

> "Che annunzio funesto!" (What a fatal declaration!),

But, in place of the second chorus, he makes the high-priest speak in a way which is altogether natural and dramatic. We must here allude to an important tradition connected with this subject, the neglect of which would weaken the effect of the peroration of this admirable scene. This is in what it consists:

---

[8] The king must die to-day, if no one volunteers to give his life for him.

At the end of the *largo*, in triple time, which precedes the coda in *agitato*:

> Fuyons, nul espoir ne nous reste,

the part of the high-priest consists, in the score, of the words:

> Votre roi va mourir!

sung to the notes C C D D D F, at medium pitch, and placed against the penultimate chord of the chorus. In performance, on the contrary, the high-priest waits until the chorus is no longer heard; and then, amidst the deathly silence which ensues, he hurls forth, *an octave higher*, his:

> Votre roi va mourir!

as the cry of alarm for the terrorised crowd to take as a signal for flight. They say that this direction was given by Gluck himself at the rehearsals, and that he neglected to see to its being marked in the score.

The people at once disperse in tumult, to a chorus of suitable laconism; leaving Alceste, fainting, at the foot of the altar.

J. J. Rousseau has reproached this *allegro agitato* with quite as well expressing the disorder of joy as of terror. One may reply to this stricture that the musician found himself placed, as it were, upon the boundary or point of contact of the two passions; and that, in consequence, it was almost impossible for him to escape incurring a reproach of this kind. Proof of this lies in the fact that, in the vociferations of a multitude precipitating itself from one place to another, the listener, placed at a distance, would not know, without being told, whether the sentiment which agitated the crowd was that of fright or of wreckless gaiety. In order to render my thought more complete, I will explain:

A composer can easily write a chorus, the *joyous* intention of which could not be mistaken in any case; but the reverse cannot be counted upon. The agitations of a crowd translated musically, when those agitations are not caused by hatred or the desire for vengeance, always greatly resemble (at all events, in movement and rhythm) the musical expression of tumultuous joy. A more real defect is presented by this chorus from the point of view of the necessities of scenic action; for it is too short, and this feature injures the musical effect, on account of the eighteen bars of which it is composed rendering it difficult for the chorus to quit the scene in time, without entirely sacrificing the last part of the number.

The queen, thus left alone in the temple, expresses her anxiety in one of those recitatives which only Gluck has ever known how to write. This monologue, already beautiful in Italian, in French is sublime. I do not think it would be possible to find anything comparable, in point of truth and force of expression (for a recitative like this stands upon the same level as an air), to the music of the following words:

> Il n'est plus pour moi d'espérance !
> Tout fuit . . . . tout m'abandonne à mon funeste sort ;
> De l'amitié, de la reconnaissance
> J'espérerais en vain un si pénible effort.
> Ah ! l'amour seul en est capable !
> Cher epoux, tu vivras ; tu me devras le jour ;
> Ce jour dont te privait la Parque impitoyable
> Te sera rendu par l'amour.[9]

At the fifth line the orchestra commences a *crescendo*, as musical image of the grand idea of devotion which has just dawned in the soul of Alceste, exalts her, inflames her and leads to her state of pride and enthusiasm in :

> Ah ! l'amour seul en est capable !

after which the recitation becomes precipitate, the vocal phrase proceeding with so much ardour that the orchestra seems to give up following it and to stop breathless; only appearing at the end, to revel in chords full of tenderness during the last line. The whole of this is proper to the French score, as well as the following air :

> Non, ce n'est point un sacrifice !

In this piece, which is both air and recitative, nothing but the most complete acquaintance with the traditions and the style of the composer can guide the

---

[9] There is no more hope for me. All fly and leave me to my fate. To friendship or gratitude I should look in vain for such painful effort. Ah ! love alone is capable of that. Dear spouse, thou still shalt live ; and owe thy life to me. That life of which the pitiless fate would have deprived thee, shall be restored to thee by love.

conductor and singer. The changes of movement are frequent, and difficult to foresee; besides which some are not even marked in the score. Thus, after the last pause, Alceste, in saying:

> Mer chers fils, je ne vous verrai plus ![10]

ought to slacken the time to more than double; so as to give to the crotchets a value equal to that of the dotted minims of the preceding movement.

Another passage, which is one of the most striking, would become altogether nonsense if the movement were not managed with an extreme delicacy. This occurs at the second appearance of the motive:

> Non, ce n'est point un sacrifice!
> Eh! pourrai-je vivre sans toi,
> Sans toi, cher Admète?[1]

In this instance, at the moment of finishing her phrase, Alceste, struck with a desolating reflection, stops short at "Sans toi" ("without thee"). A remembrance has occurred to her; and one so distressful to her mother's heart as to threaten to break the heroic impulse which is leading her to death. Two oboes raise their plaintive voices in the short interval of silence left by the sudden interruption of the song and of the orchestra. Immediately, Alceste cries:

> O mes enfants! O regrets superflus ![2]

---

[10] My dear son I shall never see you more.

[1] No, it is no sacrifice; for could I live without thee? without thee, dear Admète?

[2] Oh my children! oh unavailing sorrow!

She is thinking of her sons and fancies she hears them. Distracted and trembling she seeks them round her; answering the detached plaints of the orchestra waywardly and convulsively, in a manner partaking as much of delirium as of grief, and rendering incomparably more striking the effort of the unfortunate queen to resist the impression of these cherished voices, as she repeats, for the last time, and with the accent of an unshakable resolution:

> Non, ce n'est point un sacrifice.

Truly, when dramatic music has arrived at this degree of poetic elevation, we must pity the executants who have to render the composer's thought. Talent alone is scarcely sufficient for such a crushing task, and almost genius is required.

The recitative:

> Arbitres du sort des humains,[3]

in which Alceste, on her knees at the feet of the statue of Apollo, pronounces her terrible vow, is wanting in the Italian score; as is also the preceding air. The accent of the former is energetic and grandiose; and it presents, moreover, the peculiar point in instrumentation that, in it, the voice is almost constantly followed in the unison and in the octave by six wind instruments (two oboes, two clarinets and two horns) on the *tremoto* of all the strings. This word "tremoto" does

---

[3] Arbiters of human fate.

not indicate, in the scores of Gluck, that trembling of the orchestra which he has elsewhere very often employed, and which is indicated by the ordinary term "tremolo," meaning that the same note is to be repeated as rapidly as possible by a multitude of tiny bowings. The question here is of that trembling of the finger of the left hand pressed upon the string which gives to the sound a sort of undulation. Gluck indicates it by this sign, placed over the notes held:

and sometimes also by the word *appogiato*. There is another kind of trembling which he also employs in the recitatives, the effect of which is very dramatic. He designates it by dots placed above a long note, and covered by a slur thus:

That signifies that the bows should repeat, but without rapidity, the same sound in an *irregular* manner; some giving four notes in a bar, others eight, others five or seven, or six; producing thus a multitude of different rhythms which, by their incoherence, profoundly trouble the entire orchestra; and spread throughout the accompaniments that peculiar wave which is so suitable for many situations.

In the recitative which I have just quoted, this system of orchestration with the *tremoto appogiato*, the solemn tones of the wind instruments following the voice, and the formidable designs of the basses descending diatonically during the intervals of silence of the vocal part, produce an effect of incomparable grandeur.

Let us remark the singular chain of modulations which the composer follows in order to join together the two grand airs which Alceste sings at the end of the first act. The first is in D major; but the recitative which follows it, and of which I have just now spoken, commencing also in D, finishes in C sharp minor. The entrance of the high priest, when he returns to say that the vow of Alceste is accepted, takes place on a ritornello in C sharp minor; which, at its conclusion, meets an air in E flat; whilst the last air of the queen is in B flat.

The number which is sung by the priest, and which commences:

Déjà la mort s'apprête,

is in two movements; and is of an almost threatening character in its second part. It consists of the air of Ismène from the Italian "Alceste," "Parto ma senti," but it is here transfigured and extended by the consummate art with which Gluck has succeeded in modifying and adapting it to different words. In French the *andante* is shorter, the *allegro* longer, and a rather interesting bassoon part is added to the orchestra; but, otherwise, the fundamental thought is nearly everywhere preserved. It must here be noted that a very important nuance, the indication of which was neither in the published French score nor in the manuscript in use at the Opera, was, on the contrary, marked with the greatest care in the Italian score.

In the continuous design of the second violins, in accompanying the allegro, the first half of each bar ought to be *forte* and the second *piano*. In spite of the neglect of engravers and copyists, this double nuance is really too prominent an effect to be passed over by playing the passage *mezzo forte* throughout, as I have formerly heard done at the Opera.

Probably this is but another of those errors which Gluck corrected at rehearsal; but which, not being marked, either in the parts or in the score, naturally mislead executants who, a long time afterwards, have to play the work without the great master's assistance.

I now arrive at the air:

Divinités du Styx!

Alceste is again alone; the high priest has quitted her, announcing that the ministers of the god of the dead will wait for her at the entrance of Tartarus at the close of the day. All is over now; and only a few hours remain to her. But the weak woman and the trembling mother has disappeared, giving place to a being who, partly supernatural by the fanaticism of her love, believes herself henceforth inaccessible to fear, and capable of knocking, without misgiving, at the very gates of hell.

In this paroxysm of heroic enthusiasm Alceste challenges the gods of the Styx in order to defy them. A rough and terrible voice answers her; and the cry of joy of the infernal cohorts, as well as the horrible fanfare of the trumpet in Tartarus, falls for the first time upon the ear of the young and beautiful queen who is going to die. Her courage is not shaken, she apostrophises, on the contrary, with an increased energy those eager gods; whose threats she despises, and whose pity she disdains. Truly, she has *one* momentary feeling of tenderness; but her audacity soon returns, and the words fall quickly from her:

Je sens une force nouvelle.[4]

Her voice gradually rises, its inflections become more and more passionate:

Mon cœur est animé du plus noble transport.[5]

Then, after a short silence, resuming her trembling evocation and, deaf alike to the barkings of Cerberus and to the threatening call of the shades, she repeats again:

Je n'invoquerai point votre pitié cruelle.[6]

with such accents that the strange noises of the abyss disappear, subdued by this last cry of enthusiasm mingled with anguish and horror.

I believe that this prodigious piece forms the most

---

[4] I feel a new strength.
[5] A noble joy animates my heart.
[6] I shall not invoke your cruel pity.

complete manifestation of Gluck's faculties; which will, perhaps, never appear again, reunited in the same degree, in any of his works: powerful inspiration; high conception; grandeur of style; fertility of thought; profound acquaintance with the art of dramatising the orchestra; penetrating melody; an expression invariably just, natural and picturesque; an apparent disorder which, in reality, is an order only the more skilfully regulated; simplicity of harmony; clearness of design; and, over and above all, a force so immense as to amaze the imagination which is capable of appreciating it.

This monumental air, this climax of a vast *crescendo*, prepared during the entire second half of the first act, never fails to transport the audience when it is well performed; on account of various emotions which it would be useless to attempt to describe. It is necessary, in order that its execution should be faithful and complete, that the part of Alceste should be confided to a great actress, possessing a grand voice and a certain agility; not in vocalisation, but in emission, so as to allow of rapid recitation without taking time to pose each note. Without that, the episodial *prestissimo* in the middle: "Je sens une force nouvelle," would be wellnigh lost. Let us remark the great liberty which Gluck has taken in this passage to disregard form, and even symmetry. This *prestissimo* is composed of five phrases of five bars each, with four additional bars; and this irregular succession, far from offending the listener, strikes him at once and finally carries him away.

In order to render this air well, the degree of movement for each section must be chosen from the beginning with great judgment. A certain sombre majesty is felt at the start; this being very delicately modified afterwards for the final melody, which is so touching :

> Mourir pour ce qu'on aime est un trop doux effort
> Une vertu si naturelle.[7]

and of which every bar seems to inspire grief and inflict a wound.

Moreover, it is absolutely necessary that the orchestra should share the singer's inspiration; that the *forte* should be terrible; the *piano* sometimes threatening and sometimes soothing and tender; whilst, above all, the brass instruments should give to their two first notes a thundering sonority by attacking them vigorously, and sustaining them without flinching, throughout the entire bar. In that case, a result is attained of which the grandest efforts of musical art have offered hitherto few examples.

It is scarcely conceivable that Gluck, in order to lend himself to the exigencies of French verse, or to the incompetence of his translator, should have consented to disfigure, or, to speak more plainly, to destroy the marvellous disposition of the opening of this incomparable air, which he has on the contrary so advan-

---

[7] To die for what one loves is but too sweet an effort; so natural a virtue.

tageously modified in nearly all the remainder. It is true, however. The first line of the Italian text ran thus:

Ombre larve, compagne di morte.

The first word, *ombre*, with which the air begins, being allotted to two long notes, of which the first may and ought to be a *crescendo*, gives the voice time to develop itself, and renders the response of the infernal gods, represented by the horns and the trombones, much more striking; the voice part ceasing at the very moment when the instrumental cry is raised. It is the same thing with the two notes, written a third higher, for the second word—*larve*.

In the French translation, in place of the two Italian words, which might have been translated by simply adding to them an "s," we have:

Divinités du Styx.

In consequence of this, instead of an excellent vocal phrase, with complete sense, within the limits of one bar, the change produces five insipid repercussions of the same note for the five syllables, "di-vi-ni-tés du," the word Styx being placed in the following bar simultaneously with the entrance of the wind instruments and the *fortissimo* of the orchestra, which crushes it and prevents it from being heard. Therefore, the sense remaining incomplete during the bar in which the vocal part is heard alone, the orchestra seems precisely as if it were beginning too soon, and responding to a challenge incompletely expressed. Moreover, the Italian phrase, *compagne di morte*, upon which the voice is so well displayed, being suppressed in French, and replaced by a silence, leaves a gap in the vocal part which nothing can justify.

The beautiful thought of the composer would be reproduced without change, if instead of the words just mentioned, they had adapted the following to it:

Ombres, larves, pâles compagnes de la mort!

No doubt the "poet" would not have been able to content himself with the structure of this would-be line; and, rather than infringe upon the rules of the hemistich, he has mutilated, disfigured and destroyed one of the most amazing inspirations of musical art. The lines of M. du Rollet must in all conscience have been important!

Mme. Viardot, bringing on this occasion a certain eclecticism to her aid, but not daring to suppress the words *Divinités du Styx*, which have become so celebrated that every amateur expects them when the piece is performed, partly retained du Rollet's mutilation, but reinstalled the second phrase of the Italian air with the words: "Pâles compagnes de la mort." That was at all events something gained.

What a proud joy must that be which fills the heart of a singer who, sure of herself, and seeing a thrilled audience at her feet—sustained, moreover, by the wings of the genius of which she is the interpreter, prepares herself to commence this air! That must surely be like the happiness of the eagle throwing himself from a mountain peak in order to waft freely through space.

* * * * * *

Gluck has often employed in his scores, but in that of "Iphigenia in Tauride" more than elsewhere, a form of accompaniment for simple recitative which consists of chords in four parts, held without interruption by the entire strings during the whole of the recitation. This stagnant harmony produces upon the senses of inattentive listeners, who form a large proportion of the audience, an effect of stupor and drowsiness which is irresistible; and which finishes by plunging them into such a condition of somnolence as to render them completely indifferent to the rarest efforts of the composer to move them. In truth, it was impossible to find anything more antipathetic to Frenchmen than this long and persistent buzzing effect. One cannot, therefore, be surprised that it should happen to many of them to experience, at a performance of Gluck's works, as much weariness as admiration. The true ground for surprise is that genius should show such slight regard for the importance of accessories as to employ means which a moment's reflection would suffice to exhibit as insufficient or dangerous; and in which, moreover, may be traced the stealthy origin of some of those cruel misconceptions which, in connection with his most magnificent productions, often cause him so to suffer.

Another cause contributes, in Gluck's orchestra, to produce undesirable monotony; and that is, the simplicity of the basses; which are scarcely ever designed in an interesting fashion, but are confined to sustaining the harmony; uniformly striking the beats of the bar, or rhythmically following each note of the melody. Nowadays, skilful composers neglect no orchestral part; but endeavour to give each one an interest, and to vary its rhythmic forms as much as possible. The orchestra of Gluck has, in general, little brightness, if we compare it, not with masses which are coarse or noisy, but with orchestras well written for by the best masters of our age. That is due to the constant employment of instruments of acute timbre only in their medium register; a defect rendered worse by the roughness of the basses, which are frequently written for, on the contrary, in the upper part of their compass, and which thus dominate most disproportionately the rest of the harmonic mass. We can easily trace the reason of this system; which, moreover, is by no means only noticeable in Gluck. It lies in the weak executive power of the players of that time; and this weakness was such that the C above the stave for the violins, the high A for the flutes, or the D for the oboes, caused each of those respective players to tremble. On the other hand, as the violoncello appeared (and still appears in Italy) to be an

"ALCESTE" (GLUCK).

instrument of luxury which theatres should always try to do without, the double basses had the entire responsibility of the lowest part; so that, whenever the composer required to use a close harmony, he was necessarily obliged, considering the impossibility of making the violoncello heard, and the natural gravity of tone of the double basses, to write the part for the latter very high; in order to bring it closer to that of the violins.

Since that time, the absurdity of such a custom has been realised; both in France and Germany. Violoncellos have been introduced into the orchestra, in superior number to the double basses; from which it results that the lower part in several of Gluck's works is now placed in circumstances essentially different from those prevailing at the time it was written, and that it is wrong to reproach the composer with the exuberance it has acquired in spite of him, and at the expense of the rest of the orchestra.

Gluck has so constantly abstained from employing the low notes of the clarinet, as well as those of both horns and trombones, that he seems not to have known them. A profound study of his instrumentation would lead us too far from our subject. It will be sufficient to say that he was the first in France to employ (once only) the bass drum (without cymbals) in the final chorus of "Iphigenia in Aulide"; the cymbals (without bass drum); and the triangle and tambourin, in the first act of "Iphigenia in Tauride";

instruments which, nowadays, are so stupidly employed and so revoltingly abused.

The second and third acts of "Alceste" are, in the opinion of some superficial judges, inferior to the first. The situations of the drama itself are less striking, and prejudice one another by their resemblance and unfortunate monotony. But the musician shows no shortcoming, seeming rather to redouble his inspiration in order to resist this defect; up to the last moment the same impetus moves him, pointing out new forms; and, always with more and more irresistible power, mourning, despair, dismay, tenderness, anguish and stupor continue to be faithfully depicted. He inundates you with touching melodies and dolorous accents; in the voices as also in both high and middle orchestral parts. Everything seems to supplicate—to weep—to sigh; and yet this unquenchable grief continues to move us—such is the force of the beautiful inspiration possessed by the poet-musician.

In the second act, moreover, the rejoicings, due to the restoration of the king, cause the introduction of some very graceful numbers, and of cheerful melodies; the charm of which is doubled by their contrast with all the remainder.

The choruses:

> Que les plus doux transports,

and

> Livrons-nous à l'allégresse

have not precisely the "brio" which some listeners might desire. These pieces express a description of tender and simple gaiety in which, however, I trace a special merit. It is the joy of a people who love their king; and their hearts are still affected by the anxiety from which they have only just been released. This accords with what Admète tells us at his entrance; that the Thessalians are less his subjects than his friends. Thus the melody which follows is entirely in this sentiment.

> Admète va faire encore
> De son peuple qui l'adore
> Et la gloire et le bonheur.[8]

In the midst of the singing of this very "air de danse," the queen, passing through the groups, completes the strophe with the following sad line:

> Ces chants me déchirent le cœur ![9]

and the public joy increases.

In a study like this, where criticisms are uniformly in praise, it is necessary to recognise some weaknesses of the composer; if only to confirm the respects in which he is attached to our human nature.

In the middle of the first chorus of the Thessalian people, whose gentle gaiety, I repeat, is expressed in so true and charming a manner, there is an absurdity of

---

[8] Admète is still to remain the glory and happiness of a people who love him.
[9] These songs tear my very heart. (It will be noticed that this line accords in rhyme and metre with those of the last quotation.)

instrumentation, consisting of a horn part making octave skips and diatonic successions, impossible to be executed in such a quick movement. The poorest musician, witness of this *lapsus calami*, would have been able to say to Gluck:

"Eh! Monseigneur, what is this you have written? You know very well that these dispersed octaves and the whole rapid design would be difficult enough for violoncellos; and are out of the question for instruments with an embouchure, such as horns; and, especially, horns in G. And you also know very well that, even if, by any chance, such things could be done, the effect would only make people laugh."

It can only be said that such a distraction on the part of a great master cannot be explained.

A third joyous chorus appears to me, even more than the two preceding ones, to express the affection of the people for their king. It commences:

> Vivez, coulez des jours digne d'envie!

and is provided with repeats; like the airs which I have already mentioned as incompatible with dramatic likelihood. But, in this case, the defect of the form disappears; because each fragment, sung by the coryphées alone, is repeated afterwards by the full chorus; as if the people thus associated themselves with the sentiment first expressed by the principal friends of Admète. The repetition of each period is thus entirely justified.

The vocal part of the two lines:

> Ah! quel que soit cet ami généreux
> Qui pour son roi se sacrifie,[10]

is of rare beauty; and the words "son roi" in it form a sort of exclamation in which the affectionate sentiments of the people are revealed with force and a sort of admiration. Another chorus in dance now appears; being one in which the most seductive melodic grace is spread out broadcast. It runs:

> Parez vos fronts de fleurs nouvelles,
> Tendres amants, heureux époux,
> Et l'hymen et l'amour de leurs mains immortelles
> S'empressent d'en cueillir pour vous.[1]

and the orchestra accompanies softly, in pizzicato. All is so full of charm and voluptuous cheerfulness that we seem to be transported to an ancient gynecium; and to imagine we see the beauties of Ionia, with forms worthy of the chisel of Phidias, interlacing their divine arms, to the sounds of the lyre.

The theme of this delightful piece was, as I have said, borrowed by Gluck from his score of "Elena e Paride." He added to it the two verses (sung by a Grecian maiden) which bring back the principal melody so happily; and also the flute solo in the minor, forming the dance which goes on during the

---

[10] Whoever that generous soul may be who sacrifices himself for his king.

[1] Deck your brows with fresh-culled flowers, tender lovers, happy couples. Both Hymen and Love will hasten to gather them for you with their immortal hands.

time that Alceste, distracted and turning away her glance, says, with such heartrending inflections:

> O dieux! soutenez mon courage,
> Je ne puis plus cacher l'excès de mes douleurs.
> Ah! malgré moi des pleurs
> S'échappent de mes yeux et baignent mon visage.[2]

After this the divine smile beams again, and the chorus resumes, in the major mode, and with its pizzicato accompaniment:

> Parez vos fronts de fleurs nouvelles

This is epitomised by the great poet who said:

> Les forts sont les plus doux;

or, that "the strong are the most gentle."

The air of Admète:

> Bannis la crainte et les alarmes

is full of a tender severity. The joy of the young king, now restored, is as complete as his love for Alceste is profound. The melody of this piece appears to me of exquisite elegance; and the string accompaniments enlace it, like the caresses of an innocent love. Let us mention, in passing, the effect of the two oboes playing in thirds; and of the palpitating sobs of the strings, during these two lines of the following recitative:

---

[2] O gods, sustain my courage. I can no longer hide my excess of pain. Ah! in spite of me the tears will fall and bathe my face.

> Je cherche tes regards, tu détournes les yeux;
> Ton cœur me fuit, je l'entends qui soupire.[3]

as also this admirable exclamation of the queen:

> Ils savent, ces dieux, si je t'aime.[4]

Here the repetition of the first words: "Ils savent, ces dieux," which the musician has allowed, instead of being nonsensical, or insipid (as happens too often in similar cases with works of a vulgar style) doubles the excessive power of the phrase, and the intensity of the sentiment expressed.

The melody of the air:

> Je n'ai jamais chéri la vie,[5]

is as sweet as it is noble; its accent is that of an ardent tenderness; which finds vent especially at the line:

> Qu'elle me soit cent fois ravie![6]

It was certainly impossible to give fuller expression to the words, "cent fois" (a hundred times), which fully reveal the immense love of this devoted heart. A striking picture is produced at the passage:

> Jusque dans la nuit éternelle,[7]

---

[3] I seek thy glance but it is turned aside: thy heart turns from me, I hear its very sighs.

[4] The gods know how I love thee.

[5] See also page 70.

[6] See also page 70.

[7] Down into the eternal night.

the solemnity of which is increased by the horns, in octaves with the voice part; but this does not happen because the phrase embraces the interval of a tenth from top to bottom, or because the voice *descends* to the words: "la nuit éternelle" (eternal night). I believe that I have proved, elsewhere, that musical sounds do not in reality *ascend* or *descend;* and that the terms *high* and *low* have only been admitted as a consequence of our habit in following the notes in the direction which they take (either from high to low or low to high) *on paper.* The beauty of this passage and the musical image which results therefrom are due to the fact that the voice, in passing from high to low sounds, assumes a more sombre character; and that this is augmented both by the transition from major to minor, and by the sinister harmony produced by the entrance of the basses at the word "éternelle." Neither is it for the puerile pleasure of playing upon words that Gluck has inserted this dark tint; the pause of which, occurring on its penultimate syllable, seems to complete its obscurity; but because it is natural that Alceste, being about to die, should not be able to restrain her terror in speaking of death; which, for her, is so close at hand.

This air, as I have already said, is repeated; being composed of two periods, each one of which is performed twice, without the repetition being justified by any plausible motive. The ear accepts this kindly enough, because it is not easy to tire of such beautiful music; but the dramatic sense is shocked, and Gluck is here in evident contradiction with his own principle.

The immense recitative, during which Admète, by dint of persistence, finally draws from Alceste the secret of her devotion, is one of the most astonishing in the score; and contains no word which is not well said, and no intention which is not well placed in relief. The entreaties of Admète; the dolorous asides of Alceste; the increasing warmth of the dialogue; and the furious impetuosity of the orchestra, when the king, in desperation, cries out:

> Non; je cours réclamer leur suprême justice ![8]

almost convert this scene into a pendant of the priest's recitative in the first act; and the air which terminates it crowns it magnificently.

One can scarcely realise how, by such simple means, the music can have attained such an intensity of expression and such a dignified degree of pathos. The question was here, to blend the accent of reproach with that of love; to mingle sentiments of fury and tenderness; and the composer has well succeeded in the task.

> Barbare! non sans toi je ne puis vivre,
> Tu le sais, tu n'en doutes pas!

cries the unfortunate Admète; and when, interrupted for a moment by Alceste, who cannot restrain the exclamation:

---

[8] No, I hasten to appeal to their supreme justice.

Ah! cher époux! (Ah! dearest spouse!)

he resumes, with more vehemence than before:

> Je ne puis vivre, tu le sais, tu n'en doutes pas!

and precipitates himself distracted from the scene, the spectators have barely sufficient strength to applaud.

The recitative which follows shows us the queen more calm; but her resignation is not destined to be of long duration.

The chorus now becomes the feature of interest, with:

> Tant de grâces! tant de beauté!
> Son amour, sa fidélité,
> Tant de vertus, de si doux charmes,
> Nos vœux, nos prières, nos larmes.
> Grands dieux! ne peuvent vous fléchir,
> Et vous allez nous la ravir.[9]

One isolated voice answers another; then, the two unite; the entire chorus follows with its lamentations; and, finally, when all the voices have become extinguished in a *pianissimo*, the instruments, left alone, terminate the concert of griefs by four bars, of an expression grave and resigned, which, in the mysterious language of the orchestra, seem to say much more to the heart and mind than have any of the poet's lines.

> Dérobez-moi ces pleurs, cessez de m'attendrir,[10]

---

[9] Even so much grace and beauty; her love and great fidelity; such virtue and such charm; our hopes and prayers and tears; great gods! not all of these can move you: you will surely take her from us.

[10] Hide from me those tears and cease to wring my heart.

resumes Alceste; in rising from the seat upon which she had fallen during the preceding lamentation. After this instant of resignation, despair is upon the point of invading her soul anew; and she is silent. An instrument of the orchestra raises a melodious plaint; and is accompanied by other instruments having a sort of arpeggio ostinato and slow, and of which the fourth note is always accentuated. This constant return of the same accent in the same place and with the same degree of intensity represents the grief which every pulsation of Alceste's heart renews, whilst she is under the influence of one implacable thought. The queen deplores her fate and craves the pity of her friends in that immortal *adagio* which surpasses, in grandeur of style, everything we know of the same kind in music:

Ah! malgré moi mon faible cœur partage . . .

What melodic texture! What modulations! What graduation of the accents against that furious orchestral accompaniment:

> Voyez quelle est la rigueur de mon sort!
> Epouse, mère et reine si chérie,
> Rien ne manquait au bonheur de ma vie,
> Et je n'ai plus d'autre espoir que la mort![1]

But now the stress is about to return. Despair becomes the master, the feverish delirium reappears in

---

[1] Think of the cruelty of my fate! Wife, mother, queen beloved—nothing was wanting to my happiness in life and now my only hope is in death.

greater intensity, and the orchestra trembles in a rapid movement:

> O ciel! quel supplice et quelle douleur!
> Il faut quitter tout ce que j'aime!
> Cet effort, ce tourment extrême,
> Et me déchire et m'arrache le cœur!²

The words are frequently interrupted thus:

> Il faut—quitter—tout ce—que j'aime.

Here the fault of prosody (tout ce)³ becomes a beauty; the sobs of Alceste prevent her from speaking; and, finally, the voice, having arrived at the high A flat, reaches A natural with effort, at the words: "M'arrache le cœur!"

Let us here do justice to the French translator, whose expression is incomparably stronger, and renders the musical picture much better than the line by Calsabigi, in the Italian "Alceste":

> E lasciar li nel pianto cosi.

Alceste falls again from her seat, half fainting. The chorus resumes: moralising after the ancient manner:

> Ah! que le songe de la vie
> Avec rapidité s'enfuit.⁴

---

² O heaven! what punishment and pain! I now must quit all that I hold dear. The effort and the intensity of torment tear and wrench away my heart.

3 This is in allusion to the separation of ce—que, which of course under ordinary circumstances would not be admissible.

⁴ Ah! how rapidly the dream of life disappears.

In this piece we find, near the end, a beautiful period, delivered by all the voices, in the octave and unison:

> Et la parque injuste et cruelle
> De son bonheur tranche le cours;[5]

the effect of which seems better, on account of Gluck so seldom having recourse to this commonplace procedure.

The act concludes by Alceste alone; who, upon her children being brought to her, presses them to her breast, and delivers the *agitato* with a renewal of anxiety:

> O ciel! quel supplice et quelle douleur!

whilst the chorus, terrified at the sad spectacle, is mute. This scene belongs to those which caused one of the contemporaries of Gluck to declare with reason the composer had *rediscovered "antique grief."* To which the Marquis de Carracioli replied that he much *preferred our modern pleasure.*

Ah me! What a sorry figure such poor little creatures cut; and how ridiculous they look when they try, with their little teeth, to bite a diamond. To hear such things is enough to make the heart swell with indignation, and cause one to feel inclined to be revenged upon some inanimate object. At such times

---

[5] An unjust cruel Fate arrests her course of happiness.

it seems to me that if the marble of Niobe were before me I could crush it in my arms.

In the third act the people crowd about the palace of Admète. It is known that the queen has gone to the entrance of Tartarus to accomplish her vow, and consternation is at its height.

"Weep!" cries the crowd, against spacious minor chords:

> Pleure; ô patrie!
> O Thessalie!
> Alceste va mourir!

By a musical disposition of scenic and very beautiful character, which his poet had not even indicated, Gluck has here found another sublime effect, by placing in the distance, upon the stage, a second group of voices, which he calls: "Coro di dentro" (chorus of the interior); which, upon the last syllable of the first chorus, repeats the phrase: "Pleure: ô patrie!" like a sad echo. The palace thus entirely resounds with lamentations; for mourning is without and within; in the courts and upon the balconies; in the halls—everywhere.

It was to accompany this group of distant voices that the composer, for the first time, employed the low C of the bass trombone; which our tenor trombones do not possess, and for which they now use an F trombone at the Opera.

At this moment Hercules intervenes; the air which he sings, after his robust recitative, starting with a few bars in beautiful energy; but the style of which, afterwards, becomes flat and redundant; whilst the orchestra has a few wind passages of a vulgar sort. The air is not by Gluck.

Hercules, as is known, does not appear in the "Alceste" of Calsabigi; and did not, at first, appear in the French "Alceste," translated and arranged by du Rollet.

After the first four performances, we are told by the newspapers of the period, Gluck, having received news of the death of his niece whom he tenderly loved, started for Vienna; where the family trouble required his presence. He had no sooner gone than "Alceste," against which the habitués of the Opera were becoming more and more severe, disappeared from the bill, the idea being to *make amends* to the public by mounting a new ballet; but, although this was done at great expense, the ballet fell flat. The administration of the Opera, not being clear as to what to try next, ventured upon the reproduction of Gluck's work; but by adding to it the part of Hercules which, occurring near the end of the drama, offers no interest and serves no purpose; the *dénouement* working perfectly well by the simple intervention of Apollo, just as Calsabigi had thought. The same version also contained a scene the absurdity of which is unjustly attributed to Euripides by people who have not read the Greek tragedy.

In Euripides, Hercules does not come with grotesque

naïveté to chase away the shades with a club; nor does he even descend into hell; but he forces Orcus, the genius of Death, to give back to him Alceste living; and his combat near the royal tomb takes place out of sight of the spectator.

The idea which they suggested to du Rollet for this revival was therefore an unfortunate one; and we may suppose that Gluck, to whom it was of course submitted by letter during his stay at Vienna, only adopted it unwillingly; since he obstinately refused to write an air for the new character.

A young French musician, named Gossec, was then engaged to compose it. But, how Gluck ever consented to allow such a piece, due to a strange hand, to be thus inserted and engraved with his score, is what I cannot possibly explain.

The scene changes and represents the approaches to Tartarus. Here, Gluck, in the descriptive style, shows himself as great as he has already been in that of expression and passion. The orchestra is stagnant and gloomy; allowing the words:

> Tout de la mort, dans ces horribles lieux.
> Reconnait la loi souveraine,[6]

to pass by, when a long murmur searches its depths, and the cry of the night-birds is heard to arise among its middle voices. Alceste succumbs to fear; her terror, her giddiness and the uncertainty of her steps are ad-

---

Everything within this horrible place recalls the sovereign power of death.

mirably described, though her supreme effort is an even greater triumph of description, when she cries:

> Ah! l'amour me redonne une force nouvelle;
> A l'autel de la mort lui-même me conduit,
> Et des antres profonds de l'éternelle nuit
> J'entends sa voix qui m'appelle !7

In place of this marvellous recitative, terminating with such tender accents, they have recently at the Opera reinstated the piece from the Italian "Alceste," which du Rollet had suppressed, entitled:

> Chi mi parla! che rispondo?

They might at least have given us back this number without allowing it to cause such a horrible suppression; the interest of all these pages being so great that we should have been happy to hear both numbers. In the present one Gluck has desired to paint, specially, the *fear* of the unfortunate woman. It is not an air, for there is not a formal phrase in it; it is not a recitative, for the rhythm is imperious and marked. The number consists entirely of exclamations, irregular in appearance, such as:

Qui me parle? que répondre? Ah! que vois-je? quelle épouvante! où fuir? où me cacher? Je brûle: j'ai froid. Le cœur me manque. Je le sens—dans mon sein—len—te—ment

---

[7] Ah! love now imparts a new strength to me; he leads me himself to the altar of death, and I hear from the deep caves of eternal night his voice which calls me!

pal—piter. Ah! la force—me reste—à peine—pour me plaindre —et—pour trembler.⁸

Enthusiasm and love are now far from the heart of Alceste; the impulse of devotion which has led her to this frightful cave, is broken. The sentiment of self-preservation gains the sway; she runs distractedly this way and that, overcome by terror; whilst the orchestra, agitated in a strange way, brings out a precipitate rhythm given by the strings muted; this being interrupted by a peculiar rattle of the wind instruments in their lower register; which we easily recognise as the voice of the pale inhabitants of this tenebrous region. This attaches without interruption to a chorus of invisible shades:

Malheureuse, où vas-tu?⁹

sung on a single note; accompanied by horns, trombones, clarinets and strings. The lugubrious orchestral harmony is set around this gloomy vocal pedal; striking it; covering it sometimes, but in such way that it does not cease to be an integral part of the harmony. It is of a terrible rigidity and freezes one with fear. Alceste immediately replies by an air, of humble expression, in which the accent of resignation is preva-

---

⁸ Who is speaking to me? What shall I answer? Ah! what do I see? What dread! Where shall I fly? Where hide myself? I burn—I freeze—my heart fails me—I feel it—in my breast—slow—ly—beat—ing. Ah! strength scarce remains—to cry—to tremble.

⁹ Wretched one, where goest thou?

lent, and appears in a melodic form of incomparable beauty:

> Ah! divinités implacables,
> Ne craignez pas que par mes pleurs
> Je veuille fléchir les rigueurs
> De vos cœurs impitoyables.[10]

Let us here remark the sagacity with which the composer avoided, in this air, the use of ritornello, or even of preparatory chord. Scarcely have the infernal gods finished their phrase in monotone:

> Tu n'attendras pas longtemps[1]

than Alceste answers them. Evidently, the least delay in her answer, by any sort of musical means, would have been grossly counter to the sense. This air, the dolorous charm of which I am perfectly incapable of describing, is also repeated; at least, as to its first part. In the second, the words are also repeated, but with changes in the music. The following lines are delivered twice:

> La mort a pour moi trop d'appas,
> Elle est mon unique espérance!
> Ce n'est pas vous faire une offense
> Que de vous conjurer de hâter mon trépas.[2]

In the second musical version the prayer becomes more instant, the entreaties more earnest; and the line:

---

[10] Ah! implacable divinities do not fear from my tears that I desire to avoid the rigours of your pitiless hearts.

[1] Thou wilt not have long to wait.

[2] Death has for me such charm, it is my only hope! It is not that I would offend, I ask you that my death be not delayed.

> Ce n'est pas vous faire une offense,

is said with a sort of timidity. After that, the voice rises more and more upon the words:

> que de vous conjurer

and falls again solemnly, for the final cadence, on those of:

> de hâter mon trépas.

One would indeed have to be a great writer as well as a poet with a burning heart, worthily to describe such a masterpiece of grace in tears; such a model of antique beauty; and such a striking example of musical philosophy, united to so much sensibility and nobleness. But, would even the greatest poet succeed in this? Such music cannot be described; it must be heard and felt. What shall we say of those who cannot feel it, or who feel it only slightly? Only that they are unfortunate and should be pitied.

It is the same with the great air of Admète:

> Alceste, au nom des dieux!

for, if Beethoven has been justly called an indefatigable Titan, Gluck, in another line has quite as much right to the name. Whenever the question is to express a passion and to make the human heart speak, his eloquence never fails; whilst the thought and the force of conception at the end of his works is as powerful as at the beginning. The difference is that, in listening to Beethoven, we feel that it is *he* who sings; whilst, in listening to Gluck, we seem to recognise his characters' voices, the accents of which he has only noted. After so many griefs expressed, he still finds new melodic forms; new harmonic combinations; new rhythms; new heart-cries; and new orchestral effects for the great air of Admète. There is even an audacious modulation from C minor to D minor, which produces an impression admirably painful, and which is far from being expected; for such a transition is most unusual. Beethoven has often passed most happily from a minor tonic to another a degree lower, such as from C minor to B flat minor. At the commencement of his overture, "Coriolan," this sudden modulation gives to the phrase a fine touch of wild, almost savage, haughtiness. But of the employment of the *ascending* modulation (C minor to D minor) I do not remember any other example than this one of Gluck. This air belongs to those in which an *ostinato* design converts the orchestra into a "character." The instruments, as one may say, do not accompany the voice: they speak and sing simultaneously with the singer; they suffer with his suffering and weep his tears. Here, besides the *ostinato* design, the orchestra brings out a melodic phrase which, at each instant, precedes or follows the vocal phrase, increasing the latter's expression. This vocal part is, however, replete with striking traits which are quite able to dispense with auxiliaries; such as:

> Je pousserais des cris que tu n'entendrais pas;[3]

as also that other passage, where the voice, skipping from F to A flat, suddenly covers a minor tenth, at the words: "Me reprocher ta mort" (reproach me with your death); in order to reach an affecting conclusion at the line:

> Me demander leur mère,

(demand from me their mother); to which may be added the ascending progression:

> Au nom des dieux
> Sois sensible au sort qui m'accable;

in which the same phrase, being repeated four times with increasing earnestness, seems to indicate the very movements of Admète; who is dragging himself sobbing to the feet of his wife.

Whoever, having the sentiment of this kind of musical beauty, has been able to hear this air well performed, will retain the memory of it all his life. It belongs to the impressions of which the remembrance never fades.

The following piece, without being of the same value as the air of Admète, is still very remarkable by its special contexture. It is the only duet of the score; and the composer, who has never felt constrained, in his other works, to follow so rigorous a logic, here never allows the voices to sing together, except when

---

[3] I should raise cries which you would fail to hear.

the patience of one character permits it to wait no longer for the other to finish. This accounts for the duet finishing by Admète alone; Alceste having been the first to finish the phrase. This is curious.

The air of the infernal god who comes to announce to Alceste that her hour is come and that Caron is calling her is one of the most celebrated of the score, being a piece of quite special physiognomy. Although the middle development, starting from the line:

Si tu révoques le vœu qui t'engage,[4]

has a threatening accent, made still more so by the three unison trombones accompanying the voice softly, the general aspect of the air is that of a terrible calm; consistent with that of death, which, without effort, seizes its prey. The theme:

Caron t'appelle, entends sa voix![5]

is also in monotone, like the chorus of infernal gods: "Malheureuse, où vas-tu?" It is said three times, in the order of tonic, dominant tonic; being always preceded and followed by three horn notes, giving the same note as the voice, but of a character mysterious, raw and cavernous. This is the trumpet of the old ferryman of the Styx, echoing in the depths of Tartarus. The natural or open notes of the horn are far from possessing that oddly lugubrious sonority which

---

[4] Shouldst thou revoke the vow which thou hast taken.
[5] Caron calls thee, hear his voice!

Gluck wanted for the summons of Caron; and, if one decided to allow the horn players simply to play the written notes, this would be a grave error—indeed a shameful infidelity.

Gluck did not discover this astonishing orchestral effect all at once. In the Italian "Alceste" he had employed, for Caron's trumpet, three trombones with the two horns upon a rather high note (D above the bass stave). That was too loud, almost violent, and sounded vulgar. For the new version of the same piece he changed the rhythm of this distant call and suppressed the trombones. But the two horns, in unison, with the notes tonic and dominant which were "open," did not at all produce what he wanted. At last he decided to bring the bells of the two horns together, so that the instruments might mutually play the part of sourdine; and thus it was, by the sounds of the two horns colliding, that the peculiar quality of tone desired was discovered.

This procedure offers difficulties which horn-players never fail to make the most of when they are asked to adopt it. To carry it out it is necessary to take up a posture somewhat calculated to disarrange the embouchure and render the attack uncertain. Hence the resistance of artists who, at certain concerts where this piece was performed, declined to change their habit, and so destroyed the remarkable effect. The same thing was going to happen at the Opera; when it was decided to replace the dangerous means invented by

Gluck by another, the results of which are more striking still.

The air of the infernal god, having been lowered a tone and being now in C, the horn players were instructed to take horns in E natural, instead of those in C, and to play the notes A flat and E flat; which, in the key of E, produce C and G to the listener. These, being what are called "stopped" notes, the right hand closing the bell to the extent of two-thirds for one and a half for the other, their quality of tone is precisely what Gluck wanted to obtain. The great master probably knew of the effect of these stopped notes; but the incapacity of the players of his period will have prevented his having had recourse to them.

The chorus of infernal spirits coming to seek Alceste responds very well to the idea which one would naturally make of it. It is the great clamour of avaricious Acheron reclaiming his prey. The repeated chords of trombones and the violent tremolo of the strings, at irregular intervals, augment its savage character. The last solo of Admète:

Aux enfers je suivrai tes pas![6]

is a fine outburst of despair; only, and here again the fault is not of the composer, it lasts too long. Admète, being left alone, and often repeating:

---

[6] Even to hell shall I follow thy steps.

> Que votre main barbare porte sur moi ses coups !
> Frappez ! Frappez ![7]

to the demons who are no longer present, instead of following Hercules by precipitating himself into the infernal cave, he is unnatural and ridiculous, whatever may be the force and truth of the accents which the composer may give him. But

> Le fils de Jupiter de l'enfer est vainqueur,[8]

and Alceste is given back to life. Apollo descends from heaven when his intervention is no longer necessary, and returns after having congratulated the royal couple upon their happiness and Hercules upon his courage. These three characters then sing a short trio, in a style not very elevated, which might very well also be the composition of Gossec; and which they deemed it desirable to suppress at the revival just made of "Alceste" at the Opera. It is the same thing with the final chorus:

> Qu'ils vivent à jamais, ces fortunés époux ![9]

Not that there is the least doubt of the authenticity of this piece, which is certainly by Gluck; but because it seems a lack of respect to the man of genius to conclude his masterpiece, after so many marvels, with a page so unworthy of him; and, in fact, trivial, mean and by comparison, detestable in every respect.

---

[7] Let your barbarous hand direct its blows to me. Strike! Strike!
[8] The son of Jupiter has vanquished hell.
[9] May they live for ever, the happy man and wife.

"It is a 'chœur des banquettes,' they said at the rehearsals. Gluck did not give himself the trouble to write it; so he said, one day, to his servant: Fritz! when you have cleaned my shoes, scribble out something for that final chorus."

But this explanation is inadmissible. Not only is the piece really by Gluck, but he could not have thought of it in this way, since he used it as the finale to the first act in the Italian score. Moreover, in the French score, when the additions required by the metre rendered the melody formless, irregular and eccentric, at least it was not in opposition to the sentiment of popular joy expressed by the words. But, in the Italian score, this music, only suitable for a chorus of masques, exhilarated and frolicing at their exit from the wine-shop, is an abominable counter-sense and produces a most shocking contrast with the lines of Calsabigi; which form a sort of "morality" upon human vicissitudes. These lines are sung, after the scene of the oracle and the vow of Alceste, by the courtiers; who have just confessed themselves incapable of offering themselves for their king.

The following is the exact translation of the words of this capering chorus:

> Qui sert et qui règne
> Est né pour les peines
> Le trône n'est pas
> Le comble du bonheur.

> Douleurs, soucis
> Soupçons, inquiétudes
> Sont les tyrans des rois.[10]

and we have only to notice, towards the end of the piece, on what a comic crescendo and with what access of joviality in both voices and orchestra we return to the words:

> Vi sono le cure
> Gli affani, i sospetti,
> Tiranni de' re.

It is difficult to believe one's eyes; and the occasion is certainly one for modifying the familiar expression of Horace with regard to Homer. Here Homer no longer "nods"; he has *gone mad*. What is it that goes on at certain moments in great brains. The spectacle of all this is enough to make one weep.

I have said nothing about the "airs de danse" in "Alceste." Most of them are of charming gaiety; yet they do not seem to me to possess the musical value of the ballets of "Armide" and the two Iphigenias.

I have now to speak of three other operas written upon the subject of "Alceste."

THE SCORE OF GUGLIELMI.

Let us commence by that of Guglielmi. If, in analysing the score of Gluck, I have often felt unequal to my task and embarrassed to vary the forms of praise,

---

[10] Whether we serve or govern we are all born to trouble. The throne is no place of special happiness. Pains and cares, suspicion and fear—these are the tyrants of all kings.

my embarrassment will now be no less to vary the forms of censure.

There were three composers called Guglielmi, and "Alceste" is not mentioned in the list of works of either one of them. That is lucky for all three. Is it conceivable that the wretch who wrote the one I now have under my observation employed the *identical text* of Calsabigi which Gluck had already set to music? He has dared—this pigmy—to wrestle face to face with a giant; just as Bertoni had already done in the case of "Orfeo." The history of music furnishes several examples of the same libretto being set by different composers. But the remembrance is only preserved of the victorious scores; or, those which have "killed" their predecessors. Rossini, in resetting the "Barbiere," killed Paisiello; Gluck, in resetting "Armide," killed Lulli; and, in such cases, only murder can justify theft. That is true, even when a musician treats the subject of one of his predecessors without taking his *precise* text. Thus, Beethoven, in writing the score of "Fidelio," the subject of which is based on the "Leonora" of M. Bouilly, "killed," with one stroke, both Gaveaux and Paër, who had each written a "Leonora"; and Grétry's "Guillaume Tell," if not killed outright, seems to be at least to have been very ill ever since the birth of Rossini's child of that name.

The Guglielmi, whoever he may be, who wrote the new "Alceste" has no such murder to reproach himself with. His score is well written, in the style which was in fashion at the commencement of our century, and resembles what was then being produced at Italian theatres. The melody is generally commonplace; the harmony pure and correct, but commonplace also; and the instrumentation honestly insignificant. As to the expression, its nullity must nearly everywhere be recognised, where it is not absolutely false; and the *ensemble* of the work is altogether without character. The airs of "Alceste" have roulades, ascending scales and trills in abundance; but are very poor in the accents of dramatic sentiment. Some of the scenes seem to be so far deprived of all pretention to this quality as to be absolutely comic. In the temple scene the recitative of the priest:

> L'altare ondeggia,
> Il tripode vacilla,

cannot be confronted with the sublime recitative of Gluck's priest:

> Le martre est animé,
> Le saint trépied s'agite.[1]

without provoking even the reader's laughter. He may therefore imagine what it would be with the listener!

Guglielmi took good care not to write a march for this imposing scene. That was very intelligent on his part. Nor has he written an overture; but he offers us,

---

[1] See also page 84

in compensation, a monumental feat of nonsense in the "chorus of the people" after the oracle:

> Che annunzio funesto!
> Fuggiamo da questo
> Soggiorne d'orrore!
>
> Quel oracle funeste
> Fuyons! nul espoir ne nous reste![2]

In this place the Italian composer evidently thought he had a good opportunity for showing off his knowledge of counterpoint. As the question is of a crowd which "flies" in consternation, and as the word *fuga* means flight (but a flight of the vocal parts, which enter successively, and seem to pursue one another) his idea has been to write a long fugue, very well done perhaps; but where the question is of treating a theme, of making an exposition, a counter-exposition, a stretto on a pedal, to introduce canonic imitations episodially, and so on; and not in the least to express the sentiment of terror of the characters.

In Gluck, after a very slow movement in which the crowd says, in low and frightened tones:

> Quel oracle funeste,

it disperses rapidly; expressly to the words:

> Fuyons, nul espoir ne nous reste!

which it repeats in quick movement and in an apparently disorderly manner. This allegro, appropriately

---

[2] See also page

brief, has only eighteen bars. The fugue of Guglielmi has one hundred and twenty; and the consequence is that the singers although they are singing:

> Fuyons! (let us fly!)

are obliged to stay for a long time quietly where they are. The contrast between the two scores is even more humorous in the air which follows.

An agreeable gaiety pervades the theme of Guglielmi:

> Ombre, larve, compagne di morte
> Non vi chiedo, non voglio pieta!
>
> Divinités du Styx, ministres de la mort.
> Je n'implorerai point votre pitié cruelle![3]

Moreover, in the middle of the air, at the words:

> Non v'offenda si giusta pieta!

a vocalised passage, shooting like an arrow up to the highest C, must have resulted in vast applause for the singer entrusted with the part of Alceste. The final chorus of this first act:

> Qui serve e chi regna
> E nato alle pene,

is more brilliant, and quite as jovial; besides being, I must admit, not so tame as that of Gluck. It seems as if composers had quite agreed that human misfortunes were to be discussed merrily.

---

[3] See also page 94.

In the second act, the famous number in which Alceste is distracted with terror:

> Chi mi parla? che rispondo?

is entitled "cavata." It is, in fact, a kind of cavatina; very regularly disposed, but, above all, very calm; and even calmer in the orchestra than in the vocal part. The Alceste of Guglielmi is courageous; and has not, as she has in Gluck, any foolish terror at hearing the cries of the infernal gods; or in witnessing the dismal glare which issues from Tartarus. Her coolness attains the very climax of comicality at conclusion of the phrase:

> Il vigor mi resta a pena,
> Per dolermi e per tremar;

where the composer in order to round off his cadence with more effect as he thought repeats three times:

> E per tremar, E per tremer
> E per tremar;[4]

just like they used at that time to repeat the word *felicità*.

The chorus of infernal spirits:

> E vuoi morire o misera!

which Gluck wrote in monotone and provided with such terrible instrumental harmonies is in two parts,

---

[4] No force remains wherewith even to grieve or tremble; or tremble; or tremble; or tremble.

and is quite of a melodic and graceful nature. The third act, besides other buffooneries, contains a bravura for Admète; and a duet in which the couple endeavour to console their children, to an accompaniment which, for its part, is already quite consoled. The reader must really permit me to stay the analysis at this point.

THE SCORE OF SCHWEIZER.

The "Alceste" of Schweizer was written to a German text by Wieland, which differs considerably from Calsabigi's poem; and, to begin with, there are only four characters: Alceste, Admète, Parthenia and Hercules. The work contains two choruses, two duets, two trios and many airs; the whole of the latter being in different movements, consisting of a little *andante* joined to a little allegro, and always finishing with a display of vocalisation. This is all in perfect accord with the usages and customs of a little mixed Germano-Italian school which, for a long time in Germany, was generally held in honour. The vocal style is heavier, without being any more expressive than Guglielmi; and we have generally to endure the same features, which remain quite as ridiculous and are at the same time somewhat stiffer. The little orchestra is treated with care; and praise must be accorded for a certain skill in weaving harmonies, and in the disposition of modulating progressions.

This represents the music of a good schoolmaster;

who has, for a long time, taught counterpoint; and who is respected by everyone in his locality. They salute him with affection; calling him "Herr Doctor," or "Herr Professor," or "Herr Kapellmeister," as the case may be. He has many children, all somewhat instructed in music, and who even know a little French. At six in the evening, the little circle assembles in the paternal house. There, round a great table, one piously reads the Bible; half the audience are knitting; whilst the other half smokes, only varying the operation by an occasional drink of beer; and all these honest folk go regularly to bed at nine o'clock, with the consciousness of having passed the day well, and the conviction of having neither struck upon the clavichord or written a discord badly prepared or resolved.

This Schweizer, whose music gives me such patriarchal ideas of him, might have been a bachelor, and have had, out of the qualities which I attribute to him, only those of well knowing counterpoint and equally well smoking and drinking. But, in any case, he was "Kapellmeister" to the Duke of Gotha; and his "Alceste," staid economist as ever was, obtained enough success in the "Residenz" to make a subsequent tour of Germany; all the theatres of which represented it for several years, whilst that of Gluck was scarcely known. Such is the immense advantage of *economical* music; employing *little* means, for the rendering of *little* ideas, and being incontestibly of *little* merit.

There is an overture to this work; an honest overture in the style of those of Handel; commencing by a grave movement in which the pompous basses and tetrad progressions, required by convention, are duly present. Then comes a fugue in moderato. It is a fugue with one movement clear and pure, but as cold and insipid as spring water. It is no more the overture to "Alceste" than to any other opera; but it is healthy music, free from all bad passions, and quite incapable of bringing either blame or honour to the good man who wrote it. I cannot say even that much, however, of an air sung by Alceste in the first act; where a vocal feat winds up with a shake upon the words:

mein Tod (my death);

an effect which would have set Gluck off in a fit; absolutely fainting with indignation. Parthenia has much of this kind of thing; and, at every conclusion, she fires her rockets at you in the shape of arpeggios rising up to D or F, and set off by those peculiar "picked-out" notes, rhythmically reproducing the cackle of a joyful hen; or, as far as tone is concerned, the cry of a little dog when you tread upon its tail. But, after all, these things are faithfully imitated from some which Mozart had the misfortune to write for the Queen of the Night in "Zauberflöte," and for Dona Anna in an air of "Don Giovanni." Hercules does not roam about or "coo" very badly either, in this opera. He even rolls from the high F, of the bass voice, down to the low C, of the violoncello; two octaves and a half. It appears that there was, living at Gotha at that time, some gay dog who possessed a voice of this exceptional kind. Admète, in this work, is the only character who does not much indulge in these eccentricities; the runs and trills of his part merely confirming that the work belongs, as I have said, to the Germanised Italian school. It is not worth while to quote the two choruses; which only appear in order to tell you—that they have nothing to tell you. (This joke is by Wagner, and I should be sorry to rob him of it.)

THE SCORE OF HANDEL.

It remains to me to speak of the "Admetus" of Handel, of which I knew only one piece, but have recently procured the full score. In spite of its Latin title, it is an Italian opera; written for a London theatre by the great German master, naturalised in England. It forms part of a numerous collection of similar works, which the indefatigable Handel wrote for production each season expressly by the Italian singers engaged; just as we now write albums, expressly for production on New Year's day. "Admetus" is merely a lyric outline of the subject of "Alceste"; being a mere collection of airs, in the same way as "Julius Cæsar," "Tamerlane," "Rodelinda," "Scipio," "Lotharius," "Alexander," etc., of the same author; and very much in the same way as the operas of Buononcini, his pretended rival, and those of many other composers.

"Admetus" contains thirty airs; being nine, twelve and nine for the three acts respectively; besides which there is a duet and a little chorus. There is also an "overture"; as well as a "sinfonia," serving as introduction to the second act. As to the recitatives (accompanied probably on the clavichord, according to the custom of the time) they were not thought of sufficient importance to be published in the score, and we may venture to believe that Handel did not even give himself the trouble to write them out. There were, at that time, intelligent copyists whose trade consisted of noting, according to an invariable formula, the dialogue serving to introduce the musical numbers, and thus giving to such "concerts in costume" the appearance of being a drama. It is impossible, in reading these thirty airs, to find what was the scenic basis of "Admetus," as there is never any question of action; nor is the name of any character even so much as pronounced; the only designation of each air being that of the name of the singer who performed it.

It results in this way that there are seven for Signor Senesino; eight for Signora Faustina; seven for Signora Cuzzoni; four for Signor Baldi; two for Signor Boschi; and only one each for poor Signora Dotti and the unfortunate Palmerini; both of whom were, no doubt, only required to sing their little business so as to give the gods and goddesses time to rest. The only duet is sung, just before the end of the *concert*, by Signor Senesino and Signora Faustina; who were, no doubt, Admète and Alceste. The words indicate nothing more than two lovers glad to be together again:

> Alma mia
> Dolce ristore
> Io ti stringo,
> Io t'abbrachio,
> In questo sen.

It is accompanied by two orchestral parts only—the violins and basses. The voices have a shade of sentiment or a would-be passionate expression, rendered welcome by the total absence of anything of the kind previously. Unfortunately the orchestra plays, before and after the vocal entry, short ritornellos of frank gaiety; the somewhat grotesque character of which, far from leading the listener to any poetic impression, brings him back to the heavy prose of the contrapuntist.

As to the thirty airs, they are all fairly cut to the same pattern. The orchestra, consisting of two, three or four string parts, with sometimes two each of oboes, flutes, horns or bassoons, gives, first, a rather long ritornello; after which the voice takes up the theme. This is generally one of little melodic attraction, and is often accompanied by basses only; with a design analogous to that of the vocal part. After a few bars of development, in sections of very similar rhythm, the voice generally seizes a certain syllable (careless as to its being favourable to vocalisation and oblivious as to its happening to divide a word) and proceeds thereupon to unfold a long passage. This passage is often broken up by silences, without any concern about finishing the word. It is usually besprinkled with trills, syncopations and repetitions, far more suitable for instrumental work than for a vocal roulade; and the whole is about as heavy and stiff as a capstan-cable, the stiffness being made worse by an orchestral part which often follows the voice in the unison or octave. Perhaps the most curious of all these passages is that which occurs in the air of Signora Faustina (who I suppose was Alceste) on the second syllable of the word risor-ge:

> In me a poco a poca
> Risorge l'amor.

The composer seems to have measured the length of such vocal displays by the celebrity of the *dio* or *diva* who had to make them. Accordingly, the airs for Signora Faustina (that god-like pupil of Marcello who was also the wife of Hasse) are bountifully provided with such passages. Those of Cuzzoni are not so long; those of Signor Baldi are shorter still; whilst the poor unknown Signora Dotti, in her one single air, has none at all. When the show-off portion has duly arrived at its final cadence, a second part starts off in some related key; and, after it has duly cadenced in that key, we begin again; and finish with an organ point.

Subjected to the constant application of this procedure, the musician could scarcely trouble himself about truth of expression or character; and, as a matter of fact, Handel scarcely thought of such a thing; besides which his singers would have been very much disgusted if he had.

I have not mentioned the overture or sinfonia; nor could I, by analysis, give any idea of such instrumental music. This "Admetus" appeared several years before the Italian "Alceste" of Gluck, and may have been produced at the time when the latter, still young, was writing for the Italian theatre in London such wretched works as "Pyrame et Thisbé" and "La Chute des Géants." It is possible, therefore, that "Admetus" may have given Gluck the idea of his "Alceste."

Perhaps it was after hearing Gluck's two bad Italian operas that Handel said, one day, in allusion to him:

"My *cook* is a better musician than that man."

Handel, no doubt, was too impartial to be unjust to his cook; but we may note that, since the time when the author of the "Messiah" delivered his judgment upon Gluck, the latter has made notable progress, and has left the culinary artist rather far behind him.

To sum up, and taking account of the state of art in France, Germany and Italy at the various times when these works were written, the "Alceste" of Handel appears to me superior to that of Lulli. The "Alceste" of Schweizer is superior to that of Handel. And that of Guglielmi is superior to that of Schweizer.

As to the whole of these four works, I consider that they resemble the "Alceste" of Gluck in the same way as grotesque figures cut with a penknife in a horse-chestnut to amuse children resemble a sculptured figure of Phidias.

GLUCK.

THE REVIVAL OF "ALCESTE" AT THE OPERA.

GLUCK.

THE REVIVAL OF "ALCESTE" AT THE OPERA.

GENERAL DESCRIPTION.

THIS revival, so often announced, and delayed by several causes, took place on October 21, 1861, with magnificent success; that day witnessing a complete falsification of all the unfavourable and mischievous prophecies which had been, for some time, prevalent.

The audience appeared struck by the majestic arrangement of the work in its ensemble; by the profound melodic expression; the warmth of the scenic movement; and by a thousand beauties, appearing original and new, on account of their dissimilarity with what is generally produced, nowadays, upon our great stage. I incline to think that an appreciable portion of our public is now more capable than formerly of understanding a work of this kind. On the one hand, musical education has made some progress; and, on the other, even if only by dint of indifference, people no longer experience the same dislike for the beautiful. The majority of opera-goers had come, contrary to their custom, really to hear; instead of to see and to be seen. They listened and reflected; and, as Gluck advised of a child which he saw crying at the first performance of Alceste, they were "let alone." The Polonius-class did not fail, however, as in the case of "Orphée" to declare that the work was wearying and insupportable. But, as their plaints were quite expected, they were taken no notice of. This revival, having hit its mark, can scarcely do otherwise than exercise a good influence on the general taste of musical amateurs, and destroy many prejudices. It is, however, to be regretted that more rigorous conditions of fidelity were not preserved. The necessity of transposing the entire part of Alceste to suit Mme. Viardot, and the modifications of detail which resulted from this transposition, altered the physiognomy in several places. It is true that some of the airs are scarcely affected by being lowered in pitch; but the effect of many others is weakened, not to say destroyed; the orchestration becomes flabby and dull; and the modulating progressions are not those of the composer, because the necessity of preparing for the transposition and of returning to the original key compels a change in the sequence of chords.

This is not the place to teach musical composition,

but it will be easily understood that such disturbances (workable, perhaps, for isolated fragments in a concert) are disastrous when occurring in an entire opera, destined to be rendered upon the stage.

In his preface to "Elena et Paride" Gluck says:

"The more we endeavour to arrive at perfection and truth the more precision and exactitude become necessary; the features which distinguish Raphaël from the crowd of painters are, in one sense, imperceptible. Slight alterations of outline will not destroy the resemblance in a *caricature;* but they suffice to entirely disfigure the face of a beautiful person."

This proposition applies to every kind of infidelity in the rendering of musical works; but especially to such as may happen in connection with the works of Gluck. Let us hasten to admit that, in all other respects, the performance of "Alceste" at the Opera was respectfully exact. The singers scarcely changed a note of their parts; and the melodies, recitatives and choruses were produced absolutely as the author had written them. Some people think that wind instruments have been added to the orchestration; but that is a mistake. Monsieur Royer, considering that the strings are most important in the score of "Alceste," increased their number; bringing that of the violins accordingly up to twenty-eight; that of the violas up to ten; that of the violoncellos up to eleven; and that of the double-basses up to nine. We can only applaud this measure, and hope that its future application will not be confined to "Alceste." It will render the orchestra at the Opera richer still than that of Covent Garden in London—one of the most powerful in Europe. They also engaged a bass-trombone, necessary for certain low notes which the tenor trombones (used exclusively at the Opera) do not possess. The revival of "Alceste" which took place in 1825 was far from being so carefully arranged, or so complete as that which we have just witnessed. Several numbers were then shamefully mutilated; and others (some being among the most admirable) suppressed. These have now been nearly all restored to us, and intact.

"But what is meant by *nearly all?*" you will ask. "The musical management of the Opera speak with honourable satisfaction of their respect for the score, and pride themselves upon not having been guilty of the faults of 1825."

That reminds me of those popular heroes who, on July 29, 1830, cried out in the ardour of their enthusiasm:

"Ah! They shall not say anything against the revolution, or against us, this time. We have been masters of Paris for forty-eight hours; and we have stolen nothing, and destroyed nothing."

They were quite *proud* to be able to state that they were "not brigands." There were, however, just a few little things to be said.

REMEMBRANCES AND TRADITIONS.

Still, we must render justice to this relative probity; for, in this case, what is best is friendly to what is already good. The general spirit of the personnel of the opera has, moreover, been excellent during the studies; which everyone has undertaken with zeal and with the greatest care. The task could not have been an easy one for any of those engaged, considering that the disorder of the score and of both choral and orchestral parts must have been such as (when further augmented by the necessary transpositions) to amount, practically, to copying the parts for a new opera. It could then be remarked, by the inexactitude of the old copies, by the absence, both of marks of expression and indications of movement, as well as by the mistakes discovered, how easy-going our fathers were in matters concerning opera-performance. When once assured of a great artist for the principal part, they held everything else exceedingly cheap; not troubling much to inquire about the intelligence of the orchestra, or its chief; rightly christening the latter, "time-beater." The chorus and the coryphées sang, however, fairly well; and a few false notes in the vocal or instrumental harmony troubled no one very much.

> Les délicats sont malheureux
> Rein ne saurait les satisfaire.[1]

* * * * * *

---

[1] The delicate are unfortunate; nothing satisfies them.

This time, however, the public have not been very unfortunate.

We must say that in the case of "Alceste" the errors and defects of execution have always been greatly due to Gluck's own idleness. It seems as if an attentive and careful revision of his works had been a task beyond his powers. His scores were all written in a happy-go-lucky style; and, when the engraver afterwards added *his* mistakes to those of the original manuscript, it does not appear that the composer condescended to occupy himself with any due correction of the proofs. Sometimes, the first violin part is written upon the line of the second; and sometimes, in consequence of a "col basso" carelessly thrown in, the violas are made to play in unison with the basses, two octaves higher; thus making the notes of the bass part occasionally heard above those of the melody. In one place, the author forgets to indicate the crook of the horns; whilst, in another, he even omits the name of the wind instrument which he wishes to execute an important part: whether a flute, an oboe or a clarinet, we are left to guess. Sometimes, he writes some important notes for the bassoons upon the double-bass line; after which he troubled no more about them, and one cannot tell what becomes of them afterwards.

In the score of the Italian "Alceste," printed at Vienna, and somewhat less incorrect than the French score, we find some of the *causes* leading to mistakes by both copyists and executants. For instance, the word *Bos* is met with, frequently. But what is *Bos?* Nothing but a printer's mistake; as it should be *Pos.* But what is *Pos?* Nothing but an abbreviation of the German word, *Posaunen,* which signifies "trombones"; and it becomes the more excusable not to guess this because, elsewhere in the same score, he indicates trombones by the Italian term *tromboni.* I have not been able to make out exactly what instrument he meant in the Italian "Alceste" by the odd term of *Chalamaux.* Is it the clarinet *chalumeau?* It may or may not be.

I should never finish describing the disorder; and, in the French score, by a copyist's error, there appears a cacophony of brass instruments worthy of a modern score. It is enough to make an audience, however fond of the horrible, jump and shout with pain; and looks as if it had been written with the same feeling that it is now written of: that is with a deliberate ferocity.

Gluck says in one of his letters:

"My presence at the rehearsals of my works is as indispensable as the sun is to the creation."

I believe it. But it would have been a little less necessary if he had given himself the trouble to write with more attention; and if he had not left the executants so many intentions to guess, and so many errors to rectify. We may thus imagine what his works become when represented in theatres where the "traditions" have not been preserved; and I once saw a performance of "Iphigenia in Tauride" at Prague which, had I not heartily laughed at it, would have given me the cholera. The scenic production was worthy of all the rest; and, at the *dénouement*, the vessel upon which Oreste and his sister are about to start in order to return to Greece was ornamented with *three rows of cannons*!

Neither the musical execution nor the *mise en scène* of Gluck's works at the Paris Opera have anything in common with these grotesque exhibitions. This time, at any rate, they have given the great man a palace, peopled with devoted and intelligent servants; anywhere else (except at Berlin) he would be in a barn. The singers and instrumentalists of the Opera did not, we must admit, fall in at once with the spirit of this noble style; but in proportion to the amount of rehearsal, they were gradually taken with its charm; and the sentiment of beauties so entirely new to them brought intelligence with it. The point is that, in performing the works of Gluck, nothing is more different from the author's ideal execution than a faithful but *flat* performance, consisting of merely reading the notes. It is necessary to unite to an absolute fidelity in melody, rhythm, accents and other such features, a manner of phrasing, a management of light and shade, and an articulation, such, that without these qualities the divine flower of expression which renders these works so emotional has no longer colour or perfume, and the entire work perishes. Gluck had certainly good reason to find his presence at rehearsal so indispensable; for he alone could enlighten, animate and give to the whole its warmth and life. But he was called upon cruelly to suffer, and his interpreters exposed his patience to the rudest test.

In his time, the choruses did not act. Planted right and left upon the stage like organ pipes, they recited their lesson with a desperate calm. He it was who sought to animate them; indicating every gesture and movement to be made, and so consuming himself in efforts that he would have succumbed to the labour, had he not been gifted with so robust a nature. At one of the last rehearsals of "Alceste" he had just fallen upon a seat, drenched with perspiration, as if he had been plunged into the Styx; when the wife of the ballet master, who had constituted herself his attentive guard, brought him a glass of punch.

"Oh, my houri!" said he, kissing her hand, "you bring me back to life. But for you, I should have gone to drink at the Cocytus."

MADAME BRANCHU

ON THE CAREER OF THE FRENCH COMPOSER.

I am unaware of the kind of talent of Mademoiselle Levasseur, who first played "Alceste" at Paris; though her reputation is that of possessing a great voice which she used indifferently. Saint-Huberti, who succeeded her, was, however, a true artist; and, indeed, it could scarcely be otherwise; considering that Gluck himself directed her musical education. Mademoiselle Maillard, the third Alceste, was tall, beautiful and—unintelligent.

The fourth Alceste was Madame Branchu, whom I have seen, and who was neither tall nor beautiful. But it seemed to me that she was the very incarnation of lyric tragedy. Her soprano was of extraordinary power; yet it lent itself exceptionally to gentle accents. She sang the *pianissimo* irreproachably; this being due to the extreme facility of her emission of voice in the middle register. The instant afterwards, that same voice could fill with its brightness the entire opera house and cover the utmost *tutti* of the orchestra. Her black eyes shone with a lightning flash; and she encouraged a dramatic illusion, for when once upon the stage, she was possessed by the firm belief of *being* Alceste, Clytemnestre, Iphigénie, la Vestale or Statira. She assured me that, when studying, she had an extreme facility of vocalisation, which Garat, her master, prevented her from developing; warning her that, if she engaged in that kind of study, she would never succeed in the broader manner.

She pronounced her lines with remarkable purity—a talent as necessary for good singing as for good composing in the grand dramatic style. I was witness of an ovation which she once received at a benefit performance at the Opera-Comique when playing the part of the wife of Sylvian, in an opera by Grétry; the spoken dialogue of which is in lines.

I was then scarcely more than a child; but I remember the sad picture which Madame Branchu made to me of the career of a French composer.

"It is nothing," she told me, "to write a beautiful opera: the thing is to get it played. And that again is nothing; for the thing is to get it *well* played. And then, when you have secured a good performance, the task is to get the public to understand it. Gluck would never have been able to become what he is now at Paris, but for the direct and active protection of Queen Marie Antoinette, whom he formerly taught at Vienna, and who retained an affectionate gratitude to her master. Even this high protection, with the genius of Gluck and the immense value of his works all combined, did not prevent his being overwhelmed with insult by the Marquis de Carrcioli, by Marmontel, by La Harpe and a hundred other *gens d'esprit*. You speak to me of 'Alceste'; but that masterpiece was very coldly received at its first performance; the public neither feeling nor understanding anything.

"In France, the greatest musical merit is almost valueless to its possessor. The number of people capable of recognising it is too small; and the number of those who have an interest in denying or hiding it is too great. The powerful men who hold the fate of artists in their hands are too easily deceived; and are quite unable to discover the truth by themselves.

Everything is chance in that terrible career. Composers sometimes meet with enemies even among their interpreters. I myself once belonged, for about a fortnight, to a cabal against Spontini. When they were studying the 'Vestale' his marvellous recitatives gave me too much trouble to learn, and seemed unsingable; though certainly I very soon changed my opinion. But, from what I know of the career of a composer, I look upon it as nearly impracticable in France; and, if my son wanted to follow it, I should do all I could to dissuade him."

* * * * * *

After her retirement from the Opera, in 1826 or 1827, Madame Branchu went to live in Switzerland. Twenty years afterwards I was in Paris, and happened to be in a music shop when she came in. Whilst they were looking for the piece she wanted she looked at me rather attentively, but afterwards went out without speaking. She had not recognised me.

It is only our musical world which had not changed.

THE REPRODUCTION.

These remembrances, recalled with many others by the recent performance of "Alceste," are not altogether foreign to my subject; as they naturally lead me to speak of the great artist who has just undertaken, with such success, the almost insurmountable part of the Queen of Thessalia.

We know the extraordinary effect produced by Madame Viardot a few months ago at the conservatoire, in singing some fragments from "Alceste"; and it was then only the *singer* who was applauded. But, at the Opera, it was also the eminent *actress*, the inspired, skilful and enthusiastic artist who excited and sustained, during three long acts, the emotion of the assembly. Suffering with some difficulties of voice, as Gluck does from the monotony of his poem, both singer and composer were triumphant. Madame Viardot was admirable in her sorrowful tenderness, her energy and her prostration. Her demeanour and gestures on entering the temple, her dejected attitude during the festival of the second act; her delirium in the third; her facial expression during the questioning of Admète, her fixed look during the chorus of the shades:

Malheureuse, où vas-tu?

all these antique and bas-relief attitudes, all these beautiful sculptural poses excited the most lively admiration. In the air, "Divinités du Styx!" the phrase "pâles compagnes de la mort" excited such applause as almost to prevent a hearing of the melody following: "Mourir pour ce qu'on aime," which she delivered with a profound sensibility. At the last act, the air, "Ah! divinités implacables," sung with that accent of desolate resignation so difficult to meet with, was three times interrupted by the applause. In short,

"Alceste" is a new triumph for Madame Viardot, and the one which was for her the most difficult to obtain.[2] Michot (Admète) surprised everybody, both as singer and actor. His high tenor voice which enables him to deliver everything in chest notes perfectly suits the part. His airs and the greater part of his difficult recitatives were beautifully given, and with those emotional accents which are rarely heard. Let us specially quote the air:

> Non, sans toi je ne puis vivre!

of which the last phrase, repeated upon four high notes:

> Je ne puis vivre;
> Tu le sais, tu n'en doutes pas,

moved the entire audience, and contrasted beautifully with the tender serenity of:

> Bannis la crainte et les alarmes.

The latter, which is the keystone of the part, and of which Michot perfectly rendered the principal passages, the following especially:

> Je pousserais des cris que tu n'entendrais pas,

loses half its effect by being sung so slowly. It is an andante; and, for Gluck, *andante* does not mean *slow*, but indicates a movement with animation relative to

---

[2] Let us add that she did not take any of the liberties with the text of her part which we had occasion to reproach her with in Orphée (author's note).

the nature of the sentiment to be expressed; something which *goes*, or which *marches*. Here, moreover, the character of the vocal part, the accompanying design of the second violins, and the general texture of the piece indicate a kind of agitation which is imperatively demanded by the words.

It is the same thing with some recitatives which require to be *said* without emphasis, and not *posed;* as well as with some others, the passion of which does not permit so much breadth in delivery. Thus the lines:

> Parle, quel est celui dont la pitié cruelle
> L'entraîne à s'immoler pour moi?

should be absolutely thrown out with a sort of anxious precipitation. Nourrit (the father) who, in my opinion, was not the equal of Michot, produced great effects in this part, precisely by rapidity of delivery. When asked for it, artists generally reply:

"It is very difficult, in singing so quickly, to find means of posing the voice."

No doubt it is difficult. But art consists in conquering difficulties; and, otherwise, what would be the object of study? The first comer, gifted with some kind of voice, would be a singer.

For Michot this can require but a slight effort, and, if he were more animated, he would double the effect of this part of Admète, which does him the greatest honour already.

The splendid voice of Cazaux could not fail to

effect marvels in the part of the high priest; and he was covered with applause during and after the scene:

> Apollon est sensible à nos gémissements

and at the passage:

> Perce d'un rayon éclatant
> Le voile affreux qui l'environne.

He was also quite at the height of the inspiration of Gluck in delivering, in his tones of thunder:

> Le marbre est animé
> Le saint trépied s'agite.

I could not give him any higher praise; but I advise him to attend to his high D, which he always takes a little flat.

Borchardt, who appeared for the first time in the small part of Hercules, was encouragingly received. His stature, his robust voice and his cast of head perfectly suit the character. The compass of his baritone-bass voice permits him, moreover, to attack without danger those upper notes of the part which are impossible for the majority of singers. Borchardt is a good acquisition for the Opera.

Mlle. de Taisy had kindly undertaken the solo of the Greek girl in the festival, and she gave with exquisite grace that charming episodial piece placed in the middle of the chorus:

> Parez vos fronts de fleurs nouvelles.

Formerly, it was one of the chorus who sang this;

shamefully false, and with a little sharp voice, thus disfiguring a charming page and casting ridicule upon its general effect.

The example of Mlle. de Taisy should be followed; and, henceforth, all solos, whether short or not, will be sung, it may be hoped, by an artist. Koenig acquits himself well also in the small part of the confident Évandre, and Coullon made the whole theatre shudder with his air of the infernal god:

Caron t'appelle.

The fresh and young tenor voice of de Grisy perfectly suits the fair Phœbus; whose short recitative at the end was, incorrectly, about to be given to a bass voice.

The choruses, under the direction of Monsieur Massé, leave nothing to be desired. The singers who are behind the stage, notwithstanding the distance, follow, with a perfect regularity, the beat of the orchestra, although they cannot hear it. A fortnight ago, this would have been impossible; because the electric metronome had not then been introduced.

As to M. Dietsch, the revival of "Alceste" has been for him the occasion of a success which will count in his life. It seems to me that he has not committed the slightest error in degree of movement; and he has secured all *nuances* with scrupulous intelligence. Thus, on all sides, we heard praise expressed of the execution of the orchestra; its discretion in the accompaniments; its ensemble; its precision and its imposing force. Never has the temple-scene been anywhere presented in such a way. The applause for the religious march was three times renewed; and the audience, intent, were completely absorbed by the contemplation of that divine piece. Messrs. Dorus and Altès secured precisely the degree of force wanted for the lower flute notes, and which clothe the melody with such a chaste tint. Formerly, when I heard "Alceste," the first flautist at the Opera (who was neither modest nor the first in his art like M. Dorus) completely destroyed this beautiful effect of instrumentation. He would not allow the second flute to play with him; and, in order to be more heard, he transposed his part an octave higher, to the absolute disregard of Gluck's intention; in all of which he was let alone. After such a prank he ought to have been discharged from the Opera and condemned to six months' imprisonment.

We must not forget the little oboe solo of M. Cras in the air, "Grands dieux, du destin qui m'accable," the last two bars of which he plays rather too *piano*. Still less must we omit to mention the beautiful clarinet ritornello of "Ah! malgré moi," executed with the beautiful tone and style of which this virtuoso possesses the secret.

The graceful dances were designed by M. Petipa. M. Cormon triumphed most happily over all the difficulties of the *mise en scène*. Everything was arranged with a perfect knowledge of the requirements of the music (which are so often ignored) and with an entire taste for the antique. It is the first time that we have seen at the Opera demons and shades, costumed and grouped with sufficient ingenuity to appear fantastic without being ridiculous.

INDISPENSABLE CONDITIONS FOR THE PERFORMANCE OF GREAT WORKS.

At last, after more than a hundred years, we see "Alceste" placed almost in its proper light, and both admired and understood. Recently, many people have quoted the witticism of Abbé Arnault. Someone happening to say in his presence that "Alceste" had "fallen" on its first representation: "Yes," said he, "fallen from heaven."

But this revival of "Alceste," although not absolutely irreproachable, forms only an *exception* to the general rule. In the ordinary way, when an old masterpiece is revived after the death of the composer, it is a case of King Lear being no longer king. The theatre is the palace of his daughters, Goneril and Regan, in which irreverent servitors abound, who ill-treat the officers of the illustrious host, and fail in respect—even to himself. Should we complain of such unworthy conduct, they are always ready to reply:

"Yes! We have placed Kent in the stocks. He was too much master here, and that displeased us. Yes!

We have dismissed twenty-five knights of Lear; they stood in our way and encumbered the palace. There are still twenty-five; *quite* enough. What did the king want with fifty knights to serve him? What does he want with twenty-five, twenty, ten, even one? Those of the palace are quite enough to serve the whims of an obstinate, imperious and angry old man!"

And all this goes on, until Lear, brought to extremities by such outrage, goes out in anger renouncing such parricidal hospitality; and, alone with his faithful Kent, and his fool, in the night and storm upon the desert heath, the cry escapes him in the delirium of his grief:

> You sulphurous and thought-executing fires,
> Vaunt couriers to oak-cleaving thunderbolts,
> Singe my white head! And thou, all-shaking thunder,
> Strike flat the thick rotundity o' the world,
>   Spit, fire!—spout rain
> Nor rain, wind, thunder, fire are my daughters:
> I tax not you, you elements, with unkindness
> I never gave you kindness, call'd you children.[3]

And we; who, with the faithful Kent, the noble Edgar and the sweet Cordelia are the devoted fools; we can only sigh and surround the dying majesty of our love with deep respect.

---

[3] It seems more appropriate to offer the English reader the exact passage to which Berlioz alludes, and of which his text is really but a faint paraphrase. A strict fidelity, however, requires the presence in some form of the original, which runs as follows: "Foudres du ciel, grondez, frappez ma tête blanche! crevez sur moi, froids nuages! ouragans, arrachez et dispersez ma chevelure! vous le pouvez, je vous pardonne, à vous, vous n'êtes pas mes filles" (translator's note).

O Shakespeare! thou great outraged one; whom fighting bears in a London circus and brats in the Globe Theatre have been thought sufficient to rival; not alone for thyself, but for thy successors in all the world and throughout all the ages didst thou put into the mouth of thy Hamlet such bitter sayings as these:

"You tear passion to rags.—You say it is too long, then it is like your beard; and both can be shortened together.—Do not listen to that fool; unless he have a ballad or some licentious tale, he will go to sleep.—Add no nonsense to your part to get approval from the pit." And many others.[4]

And yet they rally a great master, happily still living, for the fortifications which he takes the pains to erect, round and about his works; for his merciless requirements; for his uneasy previsions and for his suspicion at every instant, and of everybody. Ah! he is indeed justified; this wise musician, who is also a wise man, always to impose his conditions for representation of his new works in something like the following terms:

"You shall give me such and such singers; so many

---

[4] The above is a fairly literal translation of Berlioz's paraphrase; but, nevertheless, the presence of the original may be thought desirable:

"Vous me déchire de la passion comme des lambeaux de vieille étoffe. C'est trop long, dites-vous; c'est comme votre barbe, ou pourra raccourcir le tout en même temps. N'écoute pas cet idiot; il lui faut une ballade, quelque conte licencieux ou il s'endort. N'allez pas ajouter des sottises à vos rôles pour exciter les applaudissements des imbeciles du parterre." Et tant d'autres (translator's note).

in chorus; so many in orchestra; they shall give so much rehearsal under my direction; they shall not rehearse anything but my work during so many months; I shall direct those studies in my own way, etc., or, *you shall pay me fifty thousand francs!*"

It is only in this way that the great complex productions of musical art can be saved and guaranteed from being bitten by the rats; for they swarm in the theatres of France, England, Italy and even of Germany; in short, they are everywhere. Nor must the slightest illusion be allowed upon the point that lyric theatres are all alike; and that they are the dark spots of music, into which the chaste muse may be dragged, but which she can never enter without fear and trembling.

Why should that be? We know the reply only *too* well. The tale has been so often told that there can be no necessity to repeat it. Let it suffice to say once more that a work of the nature of "Alceste" will never be worthily executed in the absence of the composer, except under the direction of a devoted artist who knows it thoroughly; who has been long familiar with the style of the master; who is well up in all musical questions; who is profoundly penetrated with what is grand and beautiful in art; and who, being in the enjoyment of an authority justified by his character, his special qualifications and the elevation of his views, exercises it, either with gentleness or with an absolute rigidity, as may be necessary; who knows neither friends nor enemies; an Ancient Brutus, who, when once his orders are given, and, seeing them transgressed, is always ready to say:

I lictor, liga ad palum!

"Go lictor, and tie the guilty to the stake!
   "But it is Monsieur . . . .
   "It is Madame . . . .
   "It is Mademoiselle . . . .
"Go lictor!

"You ask for the establishment of despotism in the theatres?" I may be asked. And I answer:

Yes; and especially in lyric theatres and other establishments, whose object it is to obtain a beautiful musical result by means of a numerous personnel, of executants of different kinds, obliged to co-operate with one another, for one and the same end. Despotism is necessary: supremely intelligent in kind no doubt; but, after all—despotism. It must be military despotism; the despotism of a commander-in-chief; or, of an admiral, in time of war. Outside these or similar conditions, there can be nothing but incomplete results, counter-sense, disorder and cacophony.

THE END.

LIBRARY OF DAVIDSON COLLEGE

Books on regular loan may be checked out for **two weeks**. Books must be presented at the Circulation Desk in order to be renewed.

A fine is charged after date due.

Special books are subject to special regulations at the discretion of the library staff.

MAR. -6. 1985			
MAY 19. 1985			
FEB 10			